Also by Elissa Meyrich
SEW FAST, SEW EASY

Based on classes taught by Elissa K. Meyrich at her sewing school

"where creativity is more than just pins and needles"

237 West 35th Street, Suite 603
New York, NY 10001
TEL 212-268-4321 FAX 212-268-4329
www.sewfastseweasy.com

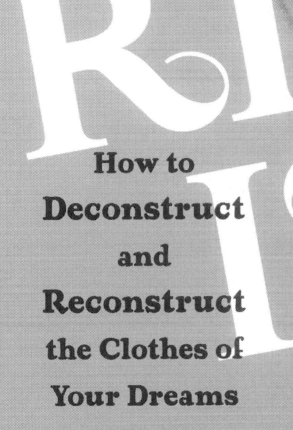

RIP IT!

How to Deconstruct and Reconstruct the Clothes of Your Dreams

ELISSA MEYRICH

of Sew Fast Sew Easy, Inc.

A Fireside Book
PUBLISHED BY SIMON & SCHUSTER
NEW YORK   LONDON   TORONTO   SYDNEY

FIRESIDE
Rockefeller Center
1230 Avenue of the Americas
New York, NY 10020

FIRESIDE and colophon are registered trademarks of Simon & Schuster, Inc.

For information regarding special discounts for bulk purchases,
please contact Simon & Schuster Special Sales at 1-800-456-6798
or business@simonandschuster.com.

Designed by Georgia Rucker, www.grfix.com

Manufactured in the United States of America

3   5   7   9   10   8   6   4   2

Library of Congress Cataloging-in-Publication Data
Meyrich, Elissa K.
Rip It! : how to deconstruct and reconstruct the clothes of your dreams / Elissa Meyrich.
p.   cm.
Includes bibliographical references.
1. Clothing and dress—Remaking.   2. Clothing and dress—Alteration.   I. Title.
TT550 .M49   2006
646.4'04—dc22   2005044767

ISBN-13: 978-0-7432-6899-8
ISBN-10: 0-7432-6899-7

Dedication

This book is dedicated to everyone who wants to be creative with fashion and sewing. It is intended to encourage you to think in new ways. Being creative to me means coming up with something brand-new or breaking new boundaries by devising new ways to do old things. Often while I am teaching, I am asked so many questions that could be answered with the experience of just doing it. Read the instructions carefully before trying to sew the projects. Always keep in mind that if you make a mistake, it's merely a learning experience. So have a good laugh and continue on.

Enjoy and your creativity will flow....

CONTENTS

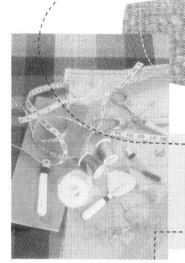

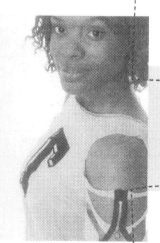

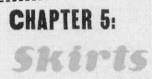

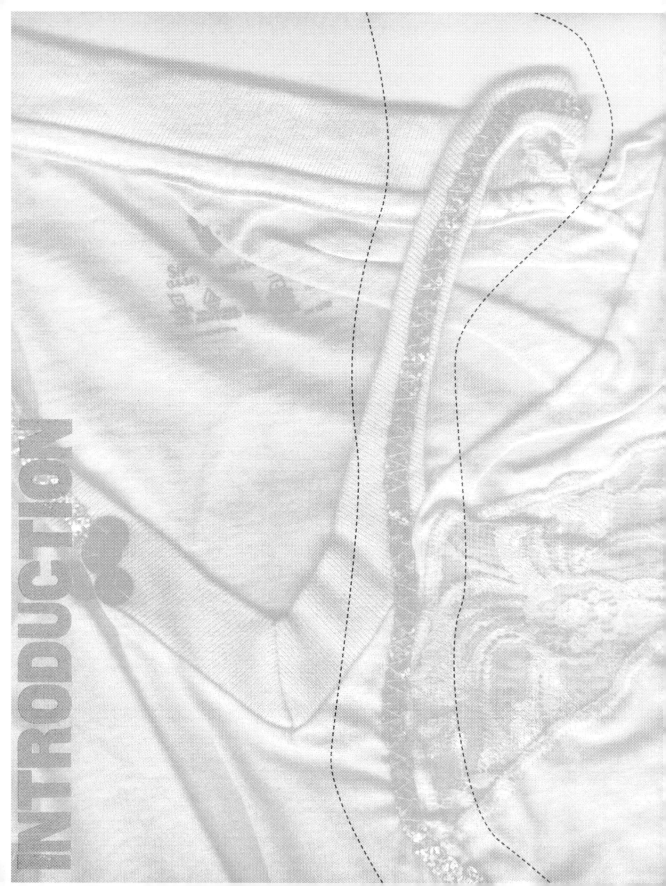

INTRODUCTION

So many people have the creative desire to reinvent their clothing or add a special-looking garment to their wardrobe without spending any money. It's likely you are one of them and that is what attracted you to pick up this book. Perhaps you have a plain T-shirt from the Gap you would love to jazz up into something stylish or you might have attempted to change vintage or thrift-shop clothing into something new. Or you have a shirt or skirt that sits at the back of your closet because it just needs *something*. This book will help you learn the approach and the techniques used to deconstruct and reconstruct clothing. *Rip It!* will free you from the frustrations of not being able to implement many of your ideas and give you a working knowledge of techniques to help you translate your personal designs into new clothing by showing you step-by-step methods and giving you guidelines to get started.

We'll start with all the tools you'll need, the basics of cutting fabric, and easy layouts using patterns; then we'll move into simple ways to reconstruct the look of a garment. Each chapter covers a different category of clothing—including accessories—and teaches you several techniques to redesign them. I've even included a resource list of where to find all sorts of trims, patterns, tools, and fabrics.

Deconstructing and reconstructing clothing is not new. It started in the 1950s when teenagers started to cut off their old Levi's to turn them into Bermuda shorts, deliberately leaving the cut edges frayed for a washed, worn look. In the 1970s, with the emergence of punk rock, fashion designer Vivienne Westwood turned T-shirts, sweatshirts, and other garments into radical designs and became one of the most original and influential designers of our time, giving deconstructed and reconstructed clothing a place on the runway.

Deconstructed clothing then moved into high fashion and became more of an intellectual process that inspired another diverse direction of silhouettes and ideas.

Japanese designers were some of the first to do this by simply turning the raw seams of garments to the outside for display. Designers Rei Kawakubo of Comme des Garçons and Issey Miyake are examples of this style of design.

Designers in New York, London, Paris, Milan, and Tokyo are all influenced by deconstruction-and-reconstruction fashion. This new-old approach and energy has inspired many to try inventing their own street wear. The desire to create a personal style and need to feel unique continues to drive this trend forward, and there are magazines and websites devoted to this D.I.Y., or do-it-yourself, movement.

Some of these D.I.Y. designers have

even opened their own shops, featuring their own versions of deconstructed and reconstructed T-shirts, skirts, pants, and accessories, often made out of vintage clothing. Project Alabama, a company known for their handmade unique designs out of recycled T-shirts that are sewn in Alabama, has been written up in several fashion magazines and sells clothing from $250 to $4,000 dollars in stores like Barneys New York! Celebrities have gotten in on the act, too—when Britney Spears performed in jeans that she'd torn the waistband off of, it had a profound impact on jean companies who hurried to create jeans with the same look. Gwen Stefani and Beyoncé Knowles appear in videos with their unique versions of cut-up T-shirts and dresses. Fashion ads are featuring rock stars wearing short cut-off jean shorts with frayed edges. A lot like it all began in the '50s.

For many years, I was a sportswear designer in New York's garment industry. After working for other companies, I designed and manufactured my own line of contemporary sportswear. It wasn't until I started teaching sewing that I realized how many people share the desire to create their own clothing. Students often tell me they want to make something that is totally their own because they don't like what they see in stores.

Throughout the years I worked in design rooms, I accumulated many design and sewing techniques. Surrounded by some of the best sewers and patternmakers, I was lucky to be able to learn from pros. *Rip It!* is my way of helping aspiring designers achieve their dreams. This book is intended to inspire and help you to bring to life some of your own creations. So let's just rip it and get started bringing out your inner designer!

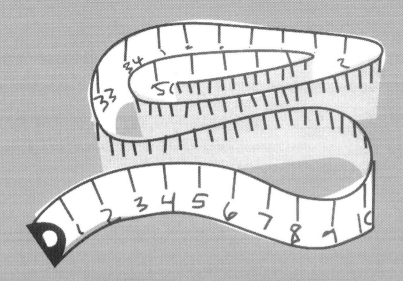

CHAPTER 1

The Basics

t's always important to have a storage box of tools, notions, and supplies to use when your inspirational moments occur. I call these items the Survival Sewing Kit, the things you should try to keep in your sewing box or storage bin. You don't want to be in the middle of reinventing your old skirt and not have the supplies to finish. This chapter includes all the necessary items as well as some extras you should keep handy in one place. Though you don't need every single thing on this list, buying them all (with the exception of a sewing machine, iron, and ironing board) shouldn't cost you more than $70, tops. Superstores like Wal-Mart and Target will have most of them, but fabric and craft stores should be able to help you fill in any gaps.

The essentials

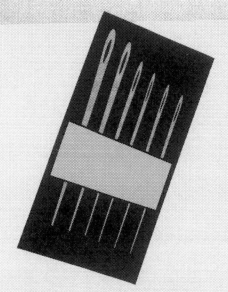

Hand-sewing needles

Always keep a pack of assorted needles on hand for all kinds of hand sewing. The best size needles to use for general hand sewing are small thin needles, called sharps or be-tweens. Use the thick needles found in an assorted pack for sewing through leather, fur, or tapestry. Beading needles don't come in general packs, but you should get some if you are planning to do any beading or sequin work. They have a very small eye, which allows you to pass the needle through any size bead.

Thread There are many different kinds of sewing threads. The best to use for all your sewing needs is all-purpose sewing thread. It has a cotton core and is wrapped with polyester. All-cotton threads are good for sewing machines as well as for hand sewing and when using the decorative stitches on your sewing machine, all-cotton thread will make the stitches show up better. If you are sewing buttons, snaps, and hooks and eyes, you should always use button and carpet thread, which is a thick thread with a waxed finish that can withstand a lot of wear and tear. Threads come in just about every color you can imagine.

Beeswax If you are sewing by hand, this will keep your sewing thread from knotting and adds strength to the thread. Beeswax is especially helpful when you're using thicker thread such as quilting thread or button and carpet thread. After you have threaded your needle, you simply pull the thread across the piece of beeswax.

Scissors
A good dress-maker scissors 8 to 10 inches long is essential. There are so many varieties of scissors available, but the longest-lasting and best to have on hand are all-metal ones. Remember, this is a very personal tool that is an extension of your hand. They must remain sharp. One way to keep them that way is to use them for cutting fabric only. If they get dull, metal scissors can be sharpened by someone who sharpens knives, who you can find in the Yellow Pages. The illustration shows you the right way to hold scissors. The longer oblong opening is for your first three fingers of your hand and the circular hole is for your thumb.

Thimble Thimbles help you to push the needle through fabric so you don't hurt your fingers. Metal or leather thimbles are the ones that will feel the most comfortable. Make sure it fits onto your third finger.

Dressmaker's straight pins These are the best for pinning your projects so they don't shift around while you work. Use either size 17, which is standard, or 20, which is a little longer in length but goes through thickness better. There are brilliantly colored glass-head pins often used by quilters that you might find easy to handle as well as easy to see.

Embroidery scissors Generally come in 4- to 5-inch sizes. These are used for the smaller work that you can't do with dressmaker scissors. You can also use them to trim away extra threads while sewing on a sewing machine. They also can help you get into places such as buttonholes or thickness in sewn corners.

Large safety pins Safety pins are very helpful when you're doing your own fittings, since they won't fall out as easily as dressmaker's pins do.

Seam ripper A handy tool that will help you to open up seams by hooking through a sewn stitch (or stitches) and cutting.

THE BASICS

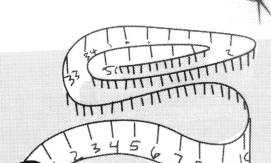

Tape measure It always pays to have a good tape measure. A tape measure doesn't replace a ruler or a yardstick, since the ruler is stable and a tape measure can wriggle around. But a tape measure is really good for measuring yourself. Be sure to buy one that has centimeters printed on it.

Tailor's chalk Generally comes in a flat, rectangular shape and feels chalky. There is also a greasy kind that is more like a crayon, but it is best to use the dry chalk when marking a garment since the greasy variety will leave a permanent mark.

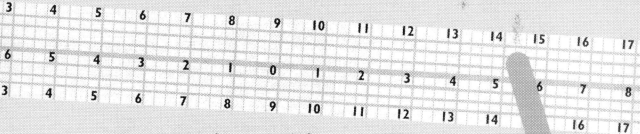

Clear ruler (18 inches long by 2 inches wide) Once you get used to a clear ruler, you will find out how much easier it is to measure hems, seam allowances, lay out patterns, and mark hemlines. Being able to see through the ruler helps you to mark new lines faster than using a wooden or opaque ruler.

Dressmaker's chalk pencils Good to have on hand for marking fine lines or outlines. Also there are marking pens that have disappearing ink and are great to use when you need to mark on white fabric.

Dressmaker's tracing wheel This tool is used with dressmaker's tracing paper to trace a new sewing line when you do a fitting or to mark the placement of darts or other designs.

Dressmaker's tracing paper Waxy paper that comes in colors and is used with the tracing wheel to mark new lines.

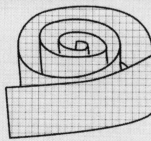

Fuse tape (or fusible bond web) This handy mending tape comes packaged as a roll or in square sheets. It is used with an iron to bond layers of fabric together and also to mend holes.

Sewing machine It is possible to hand sew most of the projects in this book and use hand sewing for embroidery, embellishment, and mending. However, it is much faster and easier to sew garments with a sewing machine, and the stitches will be much stronger. A basic sewing machine does not mean a big-money investment—in fact, you can get one for as little as $35 at a sewing machine store, online, and even at yard sales (but remember to check to see if the machine actually works). It may be that your mother has one gathering dust or a friend who will let you use hers.

THE BASICS

Sewing machines range in price depending on the features, but a basic sewing machine has fundamental sewing stitches that are needed for most sewing: a straight stitch (or a lock stitch, which is used to sew most garments together), a zigzag stitch, a hem stitch, and a buttonhole stitch. All machines come with a manual to show you how to thread the machine and how to use it, but a basic sewing machine must be threaded from the top as well as the bottom. As you go up in price, you will get more features, such as graduated speed control, different sizes of stitch length and width, automatic buttonhole, and decorative stitches. If you are confused about what is the best machine to buy, go to a store that has sewing machines on display, such as a local sewing machine dealer or a large fabric store like Jo-Ann Fabrics, so you can try them out, speak to a salesperson, and compare the features as well as the prices.

Sewing machine needles Generally range in sizes from 9 to 14. Size 14 is good for denim and thicker fabrics. As you go down in size, the needles get finer. For general sewing it is best to use sizes 10 and 12, the medium-size needles. There are also special ballpoint needles to sew swimwear-type fabrics, leather needles for sewing lightweight leather, and others. Using the right needle will prevent the machine from skipping stitches. It is always good to keep extras on hand since they can break or bend, and you should change them after two or three sewing projects since they can get dull.

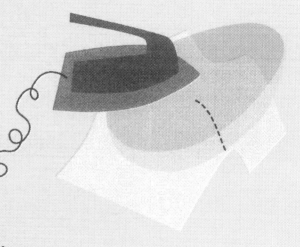

Tailor's ham A pressing tool that is stuffed firm in the shape of an oval cushion. One side is cotton and one is covered in wool in order to hold in steam. This tool is great to use when you can't fit the area you want to press on a large ironing board and when pressing a sewn shape into a garment, such as the dart you just sewed into the side of your T-shirt.

Magnetic seam guide This is one of the best-kept secrets of the garment industry and the key to sewing straight seams. Place this nonslip magnet onto the steel needle plate of your sewing machine. When sewing, line up your fabric alongside the magnetic seam guide, keeping your eye on the magnetic seam guide as you guide the fabric through the machine. A nice straight-sewn seam should come out of the other end.

Steam iron and ironing board It is always important to have an ironing board and a good iron that has lots of steam and is not too lightweight. You will need to press seams when you finish sewing them.

Extras

Fray Check This liquid is handy for keeping the edges of fabrics from fraying and good to use on worn frayed edges of vintage clothing. It's also much better than nail polish to stop runs in your stockings!

Magna-Tac 809 Glue Used by hatmakers, this is a great all-purpose clear glue that will even glue down rhinestones, lace, beads, and more.

Aleene's Glues This brand comes in so many varieties, each specific to a certain type of project.

Needle-nose pliers Hand sewing through fur or sometimes thick leather can really be hard on your hands, but a needle-nose pliers clamped around the needle will make it much easier to pull the needle.

Awl A pointed metal tool that is used for poking holes through thick surfaces such as leather or thick fabrics.

Yardstick A wooden or metal ruler that is 36 inches long and good to use for measuring out fabric and marking hems.

Fusible interfacing This can be used to add body, keep fabric from stretching, give support, or make something stiff. Fusible interfacing is used inside many areas of garments and accessories and comes in different weights of woven and nonwoven iron-on material. For instance, if you iron a square of fusible where you intend to sew a buttonhole, the buttonhole will turn out much better, since the interfacing is giving it support and keeping it from stretching out.

Elastic Generally sold packaged or by the yard, it comes in many different widths starting from ¼ inch wide to 2 inches wide. The most commonly used is ½ inch to 1 inch wide and typically comes in black or white.

Hooks and eyes Metal clasps that are used to close a neckline or waistline, which come in different sizes.

Hook tape or snap tape

This is another way to close a garment which can also have a decorative effect such as using the loop side of the tape to lace a ribbon through. It is generally sold by the yard.

Velcro Commonly used as a closure on clothes, shoes, and accessories, this is sold by the yard or packaged with two different tapes that stick together.

Ribbons and twill tape

Twill tapes are woven cotton tape. Ribbon is woven in many different widths, patterns, and colors. Grosgrain ribbon is woven in a ribbed pattern, making it especially strong.

Zippers There are several different types, all of which are used for different purposes. An all-purpose zipper is a basic zipper used in all types of clothing; an invisible zipper is made to be sewn in so you cannot see it. Separating zippers are used on jackets and coats. It pays to have a few all-purpose zippers on hand for use as a decorative effect.

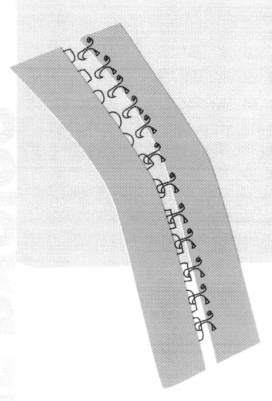

The Clothing

Now that you have your tools, you need to find the most important supply of all: the clothing you'll be re-creating! It may be that you already have particular items in mind, but if not, there are plenty of places to look.

THE BACK OF YOUR CLOSET AND
BOTTOM OF YOUR DRAWERS

You actually already have the clothing to test your sewing and design skills. How many dresses, pants, and sweaters have you pushed to the back of your closet or buried in your drawers because they're last year's style or just never fit you the way you like? Now is the perfect time to give them another chance. That sweater with the great argyle pattern and awful sleeves that hang down to your knees can be turned into the handbag of your dreams!

CHAIN STORES

Sure, they may not have the most original styles, but in this case, that's the point. Chain stores like Wal-Mart, Target, Old Navy, and the Gap are full of plain basics—

T-shirts, sweatshirts, pants—just crying out for you to put your stamp on them. And they're often on the cheap to affordable side, so with such low stakes you'll be less afraid of messing up or making mistakes and instead take more risks.

THRIFT SHOPS, YARD SALES, AND ONLINE

Shopping in thrift shops like the Salvation Army can sometimes be overwhelming. However, you can really come away with a good find if you have the patience to go through racks and racks of disorganized clothing. This can be the perfect place to see a wide variety of styles from many different time periods or get your imagination going. Like chain stores, things are on the cheap side. The average cost for a T-shirt is usually 50 cents to $2, jeans are $4 to $8, pants are $1 to $8, sweaters are $4 to $16, and dresses can range from $3 to $20. If you make it a habit to stop in thrift shops and vintage clothing stores on a regular basis, you can find some real gems, because they are constantly being re-stocked. Also, keep your eye out for yard-sale signs posted in your neighborhood.

Thrift shopping can be done online, too. There are many different Web sites for buying vintage clothing. One way to find them is to type in "vintage clothing" into any search engine or directory. The most popular site for buying vintage clothing is www.ebay.com, but there are others like www.vintagetrends.com. Ebay is usually very inexpensive, but prices vary on vintage clothing sites and sometimes can get expensive. In addition to vintage clothing, you can also find a range of sewing patterns, old and new; sewing machines; and all sorts of other supplies for sewing on these sites.

Patterns

You will not need to sew with patterns to make use of this book, but you might want to make use of patterns to help you work out your own designs. In order to use patterns, you need to have an understanding of how they work. Otherwise, it will be frustrating.

To choose the right size pattern you must know your body measurements and then refer to the measurement chart on the back of the pattern envelope. Pick the size pattern on the chart that is closest to your body measurements. You can take a pattern in, so it's best if the pattern is a little bit bigger.

You will be surprised to see that the size pattern that fits you is much larger than the size you buy in clothes, because pattern companies size their patterns according to U.S. government standard measurements and clothing companies use their own measurements based on a fit that sells best for them. Most patterns come with several sizes in an envelope. Check to make sure the size you need is included in that envelope.

When sewing with a commercial pattern, you will probably have to make fitting adjustments to the pattern or garment in order to get it to look the way you like. Examine the picture and the back view of the pattern very carefully, because you may think you have a skirt with a waistband but it might have an elastic back. The chart on the back of the envelope will tell you how much fabric and what notions you need. For instance, you might need a zipper or elastic to complete the style you're sewing.

All major American pattern companies include a $5/8$-inch seam allowance in their patterns. Seam allowance is the distance between the cutting line and the sewing line of the pattern and fabric. Some of the smaller pattern companies have $1/2$-inch seam allowance, so always check, since it will make a difference in how something will fit.

The Basics of Fabrics and Cutting Out

It's crucial to have a basic understanding of fabric in order to cut anything out. All fabrics will drape or hang in different ways depending on how soft, thick, or thin they are and from what fiber they are made. They each have their own personality.

Fabric is divided into three categories; woven, knit, and nonwoven. Woven fabrics are made with yarns that were spun from fibers. Fibers are either natural, such as cotton, or manmade, such as polyester. Woven fabrics, which are used in jeans and khakis, are created on a loom by interlacing the warp and weft yarns to form the fabric. Knits, like sweaters, T-shirts, or sweatshirts, are made on knitting machines and are interlooped together to form the knit. Nonwovens are vinyl, plastics, leather, and felt.

knit fabric

woven fabric

All of these fabrics have a different feel. When you buy fabric, handle it and feel it to see if you like it for your project. By doing this you will get a feeling for the fabric.

HOW FABRIC IS MEASURED

Fabric is measured by the yard as it comes off the bolt or by its running length. Most fabrics are either 45-inches wide or 60-inches wide, but you might find exceptions, such as some silks that are 47 inches wide or other odd widths.

Knits are also measured by the yard, and sometimes you can find a knit that was knitted into a tube and is not open on either end of the fabric. Leather is always measured and priced by the square foot. You usually have to buy a skin, and skins vary in size.

There are some definitions you'll need to know in order to discuss and work with fabric. For example, if you have little or no sewing experience you probably are not aware of how important it is to know about grainlines, which really affect how a garment hangs. No matter what you are sewing, you need to have a simple understanding of how the grain of fabric will affect what you want to create. Most garments are cut so the lengthwise grain of the fabric is running from the top of the garment to the bottom. This is because the length of a fabric is the strongest.

Most fabrics are either 45-inches wide or 60-inches wide

So before you cut out a project it is important to detect the direction of your fabric. Here's how to do this through a few important terms:

Selvage Look for this first. The selvage runs along the length of the fabric on both edges and looks like a band of thicker fabric. Sometimes it will have poke holes in it, and if it's a print there will generally be a white band on both edges of the running length.

Warp Now that you've found the selvage, you can find the warp. These are the threads that run the lengthwise direction of your fabric, and are the strongest part of the fabric.

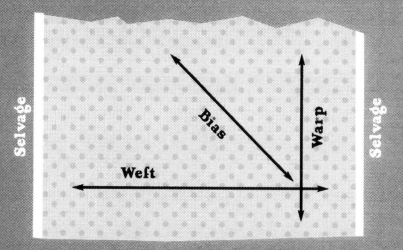

Weft The weft threads run crosswise from selvage to selvage and are not quite as strong as the warp.

Bias This is used to describe any diagonal across fabric. Bias always hang very softly and drapey. True bias is created only by a 45-degree angle from the fabric's straight grain. Generally, the bias will use more fabric, but it is great for making piping, ruffles, fabric flowers, and very drapey skirts or dresses.

BASIC LAYOUTS FOR CUTTING FABRIC.

These are the layouts that you will need to know when you are about to cut out any sewing project.

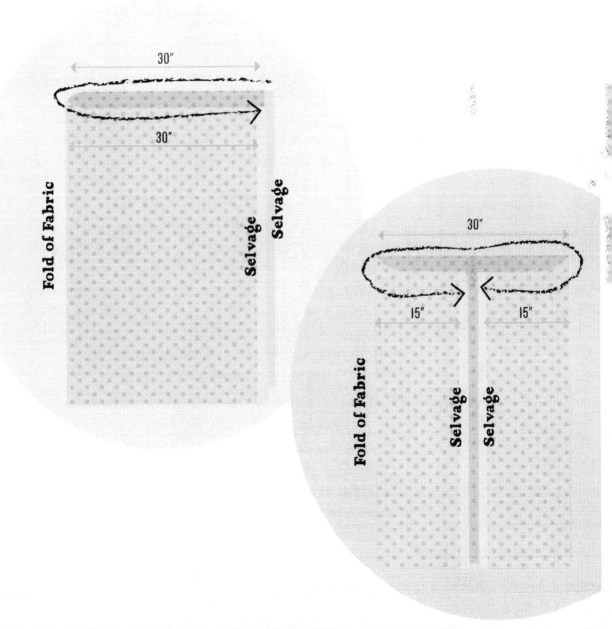

SEWING SYMBOLS YOU SHOULD KNOW WHEN USING COMMERCIAL PATTERNS OR MAKING YOUR OWN

Straight grain This symbol means that the pattern piece should be placed parallel to the selvage or fold of the fabric.

Place on fold This symbol means the pattern piece is pinned to the fold line of the fabric.

Notches This symbol indicates matching points on pattern pieces. Notches can be a very important guide to sewing the pieces of one pattern to another.

Cutting lines Patterns have different cutting lines for each size. Make sure to cut on the line that matches the size of the pattern you are using.

THE BASICS

TEN STEPS TO EASY CUTTING SUCCESS

Use this method for cutting out a sewing pattern, your own pattern, appliqué pieces, extra pieces of fabric to add on to your skirt or jeans, or any new design piece.

1. *Press out your fabric using steam if it is very wrinkled. Use a dry iron on your pattern if it is very creased.*

2. *Always examine the pattern pieces to find out how many of each piece must be cut. (The pattern piece will say to cut one, two, or four.) Examine the grainlines on your pattern to see if some of the pieces should be placed on the fold and some on the straight grain of the fabric. If you made your own pattern, plan your pieces the same way.*

3. *Check the basic layout on page 24 to choose one that works for your project.*

4. *Lay out fabric by always folding the right side of the fabric inward so that it is on the inside of the folded fabric. The only exceptions are velvet and suede fabrics. They should be folded the opposite way; otherwise they will be very hard to lay flat because they have nap that causes the fabric to stick together.*

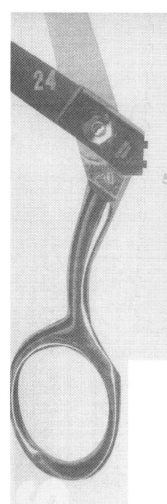

5. *When folding fabric, either make sure the edges are placed selvage on top of selvage or measured so that the folded-over side is equal distance from the selvage (see p. 21). Fabric must be lying evenly and on the straight grain. It is helpful to lay out fabric along the length of a table. There should be no ripples.*

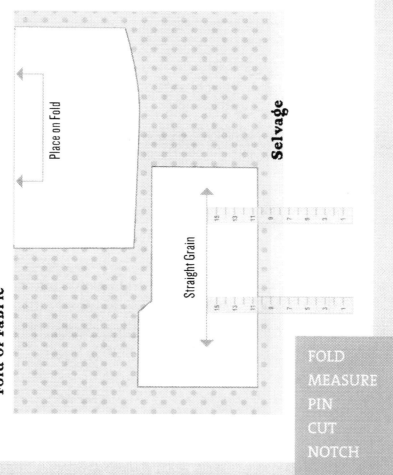

Place on Fold

Selvage

Straight Grain

Fold of Fabric

FOLD
MEASURE
PIN
CUT
NOTCH

6. It is very important to pin the pattern pieces onto the fabric making sure to follow the grainlines marked on the pattern. Lay out the pattern pieces so that the straight grainlines are always pinned parallel to the selvage, and the pattern pieces that are marked center front fold are pinned to the fold line. Use a ruler to measure from the straight grainline to the selvage of the fabric. Make sure each end of the straight grainline is measuring the same distance to the selvage. When pinning patterns down, be sure to pin through all layers.

7. Begin cutting, making sure to cut your pieces as evenly as possible. If you cut out evenly it will make it much easier to sew your pattern pieces together. Take small snips, using the tips of your scissors.

8. While cutting, never move the pinned pattern pieces or the fabric, and never slide your hand under the fabric.

9. Look for all the notches on the pattern pieces and check to make sure that you clip all of them with the tips of your scissors.

10. For fabrics that look the same on both the right and wrong sides, mark an X with tailor's chalk onto the wrong side of the fabric pattern piece to indicate that it is the wrong side of your fabric.

Fabric and Sewing Machines

When working with some fabrics, you will need to change the needle and/or sewing foot on your machine to keep stitches from skipping and getting loopy or stuck. For example, when you are sewing leather, you will need to change to a leather needle *and* change the sewing machine foot to a Teflon-coated or roller foot to keep the leather from sticking to the machine. On the other side of the spectrum, if you are sewing on a swimwear fabric like spandex, you'll have to change your needle to a special ballpoint one to keep the machine from skipping stitches. It is always a surprise to find out how easy or difficult a fabric will react when you begin to sew on it, so try sewing on a scrap first.

Basic Hand-Sewing Stitches

Some simple skills of how to sew by hand will always be useful for repairing clothing, sewing on buttons or snaps, and other sewing projects. When you have a small opening on a seam, quick hand sewing can save the life of a garment, and it is easier to machine sew certain areas of a project together if you hand baste it in place first.

Hand basting Basting is a temporary stitch that will hold two or more layers of fabric in place. Thread a needle with a one-yard length of thread and make a knot on one end. Push your needle through all the pieces you want to hold together up to one side and then bring it back down to the other side making each stitch no longer than ½ inch in length. Keep going until the pieces of fabric are held together. To end the basting go back over your last stitch one or two times.

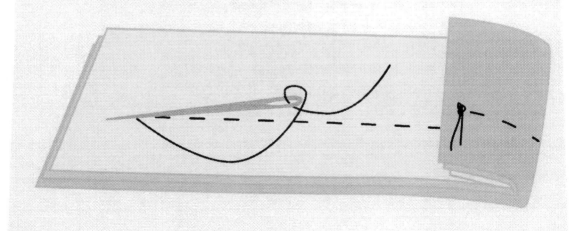

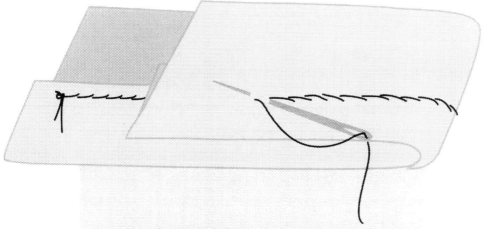

Backstitch Backstitches are small stitches that meet on the top side of the fabric and overlap on the underside. It is a good stitch to use in replacement of a sewing machine stitch. Thread the needle and make a knot at the end of the thread. Push your needle through the fabric pieces starting on the underside and coming up to the top side. Go back into the fabric to create the first stitch, making a ½-inch long stitch on the top side and then under and come up ½ inch in front of first stitch on the top side. Continue to do this to create stitches that are right next to each other and no longer than ½ inch. This is a good stitch to use when mending a small seam opening on a sweater, T-shirt, or other clothing.

THE BASICS

Hand hemming A blind hem is used to sew a hem so the stitches do not show on the right side of the garment. Thread your needle and knot the end of your thread. Start sewing by bringing the needle up through the top of the hem, making sure the knot is secure. Slant the needle on an angle and pick up three threads of the fabric that the hem is being sewn down to and then sew back through the hem. Keep making these stitches ⅜-inch apart. To end off the sewing thread, sew back over the last stitch one or two times.

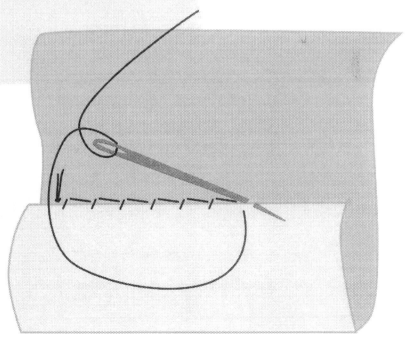

Sewing on a button There are two types of buttons: buttons that have holes to sew through and buttons with a shank that allows the button to stand on the fabric when sewn. The shank allows the button to close without pulling. Buttons that just have holes need a thread shank. For buttons, snaps, and hooks, sew with a heavier thread called button and carpet thread or use several lengths of all-purpose thread. Knot the end of the thread and start sewing from the underside of the fabric to the top. Holding the button away from the fabric, come up and down through the holes in the button, allowing some slack in the thread, which will create a shank.

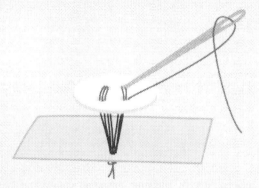

To finish, sew the thread through to the right side behind the button, wind the thread tightly around the slackened thread that attaches the button, and end securely.

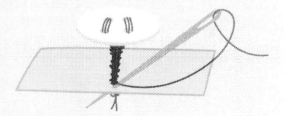

Sewing on snaps or hooks Mark the place on both sides of the garment where the center of the snap or hook will be placed. The knob section of the snap faces out. Both snaps and hooks have holes to go through. Start by sewing from the underside of the fabric that the snap will be sewn to. Sew through the snap or hook hole at least three times, then go to the underside of the fabric and go up to the next loop or hook. End off the sewing thread by sewing back in the same place at least two times on the underside of the fabric where you began.

CHAPTER 2

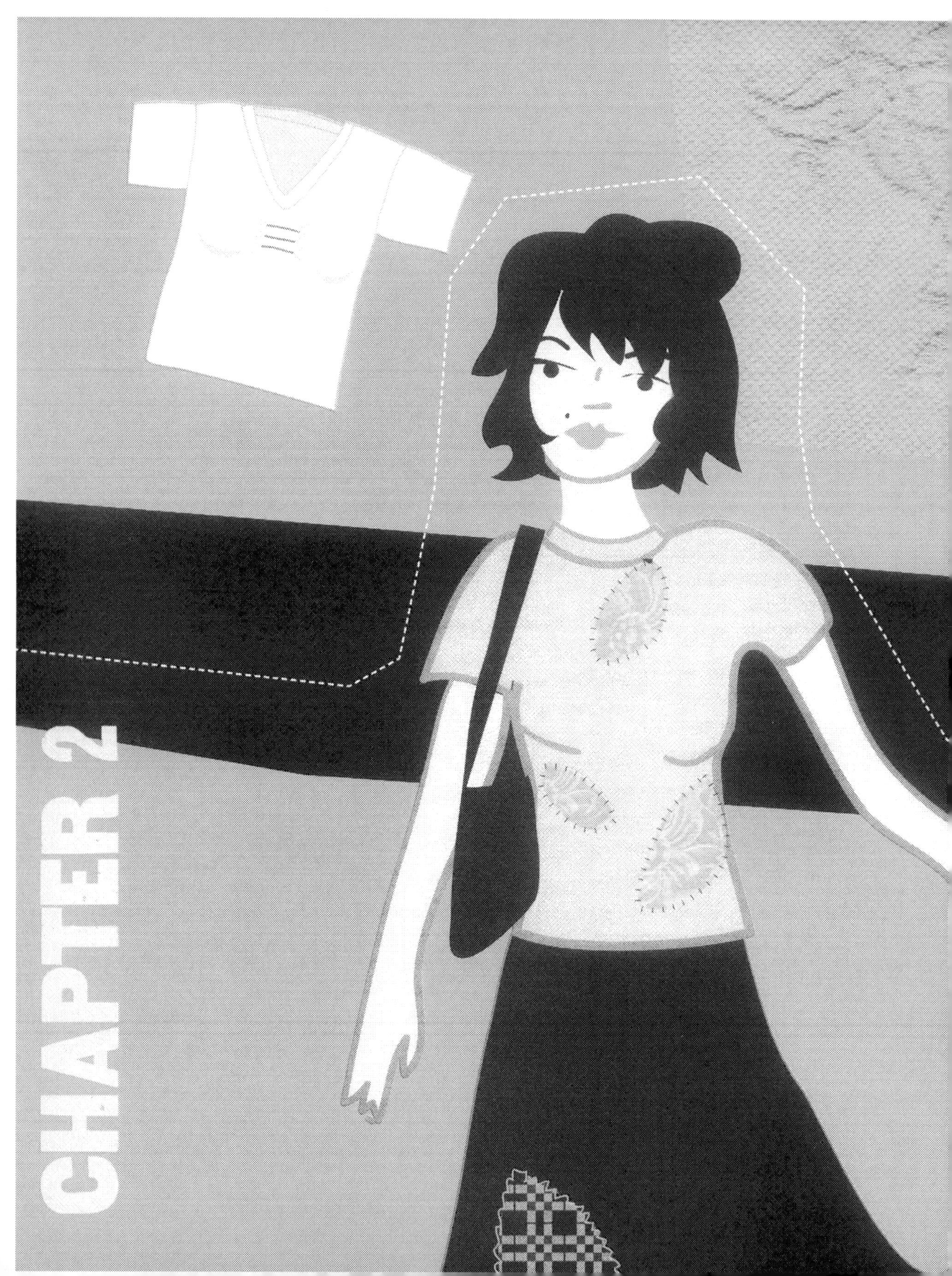

T-Shirts

darts, see page 42

slicing and cutting, see page 48

decorative zipper, see page 57

One of the easiest ways of expressing your own design abilities is with T-shirts. This chapter will give you the basics for tailoring your own exciting fit as well as how to go about all sorts of embellishment techniques that work really well when creating unique T-shirt designs. T-shirt designing has been one of the greatest social statements of our time. It encapsulates politics, sex, art, crafts, and street style.

The T-shirt has a history all its own. The first authentic T-shirt dates back to 1913 and was adopted by the U.S. Navy in its traditional crewneck, short-sleeve, white cotton version. It is truly one of the only pieces of clothing, besides basic blue jeans, that has been around an entire century and that we still wear in its traditional form today. It is the biggest anti–status symbol that anyone can wear. However, once you add special artwork or a social or political statement into the design, it gives the shirt a special, status-like appeal. There is no end to what you can create or how you can reinvent a T-shirt. I see new possibilities every day on the street and in magazines. Experiment with these different techniques to get you into the art of T-shirt designing.

The first thing you need to do is pick out your T-shirt. If you are nervous about ruining one of your one-of-kind collected T-shirts, I recommend starting with a plain white undershirt. Basic men's underwear crewnecks or V-necks, such as the ones made by Jockey or Fruit of the Loom, are made out of a fine cotton jersey knit. They generally come three to a package and can be purchased anywhere. Other sources for cheap T-shirts to experiment on are the Gap, Old Navy, Target, Wal-Mart, your dad/brother/boyfriend's dresser (ask first!), or thrift shops.

Getting Inspiration

Form a picture in your mind of an idea of the kind of T-shirt you want to create. Besides just slicing up the T-shirt, you can do so many different things to make your T-shirt new and different. Try to roughly sketch an idea. Fashion magazines or music magazines are great sources of ideas, or maybe a particular political or social theme will get you going. Also, keep your eyes open to color combinations you like, which can help you arrange colors for pieces of fabric to add to your T-shirt.

Basic Fitting and Shaping Techniques for T-Shirts

T-SHIRT MATERIALS:

- safety pins
- medium-size, dress-maker's straight pins (size 17)
- marking chalk or a pencil
- Scotch tape or 1/4-inch masking tape to mark the placement of your cutting lines and neckline
- clear see-through ruler, 18 inches long by 2-inches wide
- scissors
- needle and thread that match your fabric
- sewing machine
- iron and ironing board

ASSESSING YOUR T-SHIRT FIT

The most common problem with using generic undershirts is they might be too big on your torso and the underarm can be too low. The sleeves may be too big as well. If you do not want to spend time fitting a T-shirt, then start with one that already has a fit you like.

The first thing you should do when customizing your own style of T-shirt is check the fit. Try on the T-shirt while facing a mirror to see how it looks and how you want it to look.

The questions you should ask yourself are: Is the body of the T-shirt too loose or too long? Are the sleeves too loose or too long? Is the neckline too high or too low?

DOING A FITTING

1. *Put on the T-shirt so it is centered and hanging properly on your body.*

2. *With safety pins in hand, pinch in the side seams on each side of the T-shirt to make the fit closer to your body. Try to pinch in even amounts of excess on each side. Safety pin in this excess on both sides. You can continue pinching out the excess up under the arm and on the sleeve.*

3. *If the neckline on the T-shirt is too low, the best way to raise it is by raising the shoulder line of the T-shirt. While looking in the mirror, pinch up on the shoulder line of the T-shirt. You can use dressmaker's straight pins for the shoulder lines. At the top of the sleeve on your shoulder, start with nothing and begin to pinch in more going toward your neckline.*

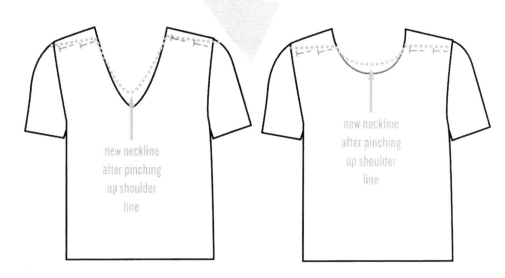

new neckline after pinching up shoulder line

new neckline after pinching up shoulder line

4. If you want to change the style of the neckline, you
    can mark out a new line by looking in the mirror to
    decide where you want it to be. You can also create
    various necklines by starting with a crewneck
    T-shirt. Take your masking tape and cut a piece ap-
    proximately 12 inches long. Start by pressing the
    tape down at your shoulder line, continuing around
    the front of your T-shirt, forming a curve to create
    your new neckline. If you do not like the curve, keep
    lifting the tape
    and changing the
    shape until you
    get a neckline
    you like. Other-
    wise, you can
    draw out a new
    neckline with
    your marking
    chalk.

5. *If you want to create a more sculptured look, now is a good time to put in darts at your bustline. Darts are stitched fabric folds that come to a point.*

Darts are used to create shape around curves like sculpting in cloth. They are a helpful way to give a shapely or sexy look to your T-shirt. The most obvious place to put a dart is starting from the side seams at your bustline. When your arms are at your side, look at the side of the T-shirt near your bust area.

If you see a big gapping of fabric, you can turn it into several bust darts or one dart. Pinch this excess area to form a point that ends at your bustline using your safety pins to hold it in place. You can experiment and create one or more darts coming from the side seams. You can create darts starting at the shoulder seam and ending above your bustline. Another way to do this is to create two long, vertical front darts that start from below your waistline and run parallel up to your bust points. This kind of dart will give you the opportunity to make a more shapely fit and it will tighten the waist a little more, even if you might have taken in the side seams. You can also place darts right at the center of your cleavage pointing out toward your bust points.

how to make a dart

1. On wrong side or right side of T-shirt pinch a triangle of fabric on either side of bust until it fits the way you like

2. Pin pinched triangle closed

3. Open side seams to add darts

4. Use chalk to rub a mark along both sides of pinned seam

5. Remove pins and sew chalk lines together to form dart

6. Turn shirt right-side out to see sewn darts

vertical darts

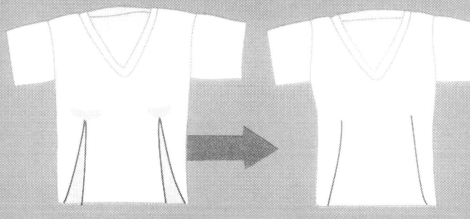

1. Pinch and pin to get the desired fit you like

2. Mark and sew as shown on previous pages

center darts

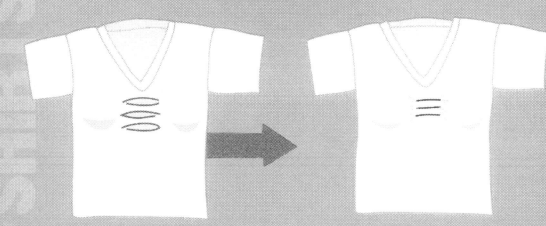

1. Pinch the thickest part of the dart in the center and taper out to a point

2. Mark and sew as shown on previous pages

6. *If the T-shirt sleeves and body are too long, bend them under to a length you like. With your pins or marking chalk, lightly mark the new length.*

Keep in mind that these marks and the safety-pinned seams should be corrected or improved when you take off the T-shirt and place it on a table. When marking the neckline or any style lines, you only have to create the line on one side of the T-shirt, because when you take it off you can copy this line to the other side of the T-shirt. This will make the neck-line symmetrical and even.

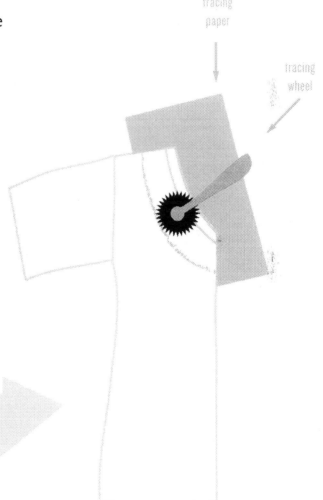

tracing
paper

tracing
wheel

CORRECTING YOUR FITTING

1. *Turn the T-shirt inside out and lay it down on a table.*

2. *With your marking chalk, rub against the safety pins on the side seams. Make sure to mark all of the safety pins, and then turn the T-shirt right side out so that you can re-move them.*

3. *After removing the safety pins, turn the T-shirt back to the wrong side, and you will see your chalk marks. These chalk marks will form your new taper line.*

4. *With your clear ruler or free hand, draw a line con-necting the marks. This is your sewing line to take in the T-shirt. If you have darts, make sure to carefully mark them as well.*

5. Now cut the T-shirt to form front and back side seams. This will make it possible to extend the dart so that the deeper part starts from the side seams and is sewn to taper to a point, stopping just before your bust point.

6. Begin by first sewing the darts you marked. Then sew the newly marked lines for the side seams.

7. Now try on the T-shirt on the right side. If you are satisfied with the fit, take off the T-shirt and turn it inside out again.

8. From the sewing line, mark a ½-inch seam allowance and then cut the excess fabric away so the T-shirt will fit better and feel more comfortable when you wear it.

9. If the side seams' fit is too tight after sewing, you have to make the side seams looser. If the fit is too loose, you can take the seams in a little more. Doing a fitting is trial and error until you are satisfied with the fit.

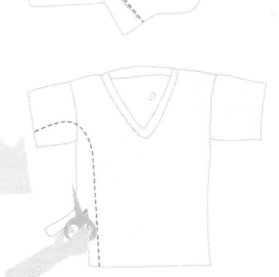

Slicing and Cutting as a Styling Technique

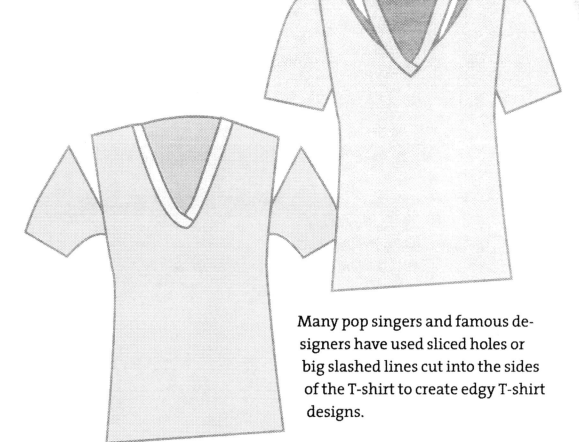

Many pop singers and famous designers have used sliced holes or big slashed lines cut into the sides of the T-shirt to create edgy T-shirt designs.

1. *In front of the mirror, put on your T-shirt to see where you want to make the slashed lines or cut holes.*

2. *With your masking tape, mark tape lines where you are going to cut into the T-shirt. The masking tape that can be removed will free you up to be able to experiment and decide which is a nice placement for all the slice lines.*

3. *Mark as many lines to slice as you like and then take off your T-shirt.*

4. *With your marking chalk, mark the placement of your tape lines.*

5. *Remove the tape and then use sharp scissors to cut the slash marks.*

OTHER WAYS TO CUT THE T-SHIRT ARE:

- Cut the sleeve away from the shoulder seam on one or both sides so it exposes the shoulder bone. The sleeve will drop and drape on the upper arm.

- Cut the ribbing completely off the neckline or just cut the ribbing away from the body of the T-shirt while leaving a little bit sewn onto the body at the neckline in different places.

- Cut the bottom of the T-shirt into different lengths or fringe it.

- Cut the sleeves shorter, cut them off completely, or fringe them.

Of course, there are many other ways to slice, dice, and cut. Be innovative—just try whatever you think might work.

Inserting Pieces of Interesting Fabric

Inserting fabrics like lace, chiffon, or mesh are another way to create interesting designs on your T-shirt. Cutting pieces and arranging them makes all the difference in how a design will look. For this kind of design technique, it is helpful to visualize and plan an idea of how you want the inserts to look. Saving pictures of styles from magazines can help your inspiration or just drawing your own ideas from your head. Make sure to take into consideration the size and proportion of your inserts and how it will look on your T-shirt.

There are two ways of going about making your shapes for the lace inserts. You can either use your chalk to draw a free-hand shape right on the lace and then cut it out, or draw the shapes for your inserts on a piece of paper.

T-SHIRT MATERIALS

- preferably 1 yard of interesting fabrics such as lace, sheers, tulle, organdy, chiffon, or mesh knits to make the contrast with the plain T-shirt interesting
- bond paper for your insert patterns
- straight pins
- marking chalk or pencil
- sharp scissors or embroidery scissors
- thread to match your fabric
- sewing machine
- needles if hand sewing

1. *Create patterns for your inserts using bond paper. Put your T-shirt on in order to mark the placement you want for lace inserts. Stand in front of a mirror and try pinning the pattern on different areas of the T-shirt. Pin several different arrangements until you arrive at the one you like best.*

2. *After you have decided on the placement of your pattern pieces, take off the T-shirt and carefully chalk out the outline of the pieces on the front of the T-shirt.*

3. Cut pieces of the insert fabric big enough to cover the outline that you have marked. It should be at least 1 inch bigger than your pattern on all sides.

4. Slip the inserts onto the wrong side of the T-shirt and line them up very carefully inside the chalk outlines marked. Also, make sure that the inserts are facing right side up. Use straight pins to pin the pieces in place on the right side of the T-shirt.

5. With your sewing machine and a scrap piece of the insert and T-shirt fabric, test out a small zigzag stitch. You should adjust your zigzag width and length to glide over the fabric and not create puckers. The closer the zigzag stitch the more chance of puckering. If you are doing this by hand, you should use a backstitch.

Carefully sew and follow the chalk lines you have made on the right side of your T-shirt. Sew slowly, since you are going to have to turn and guide your fabric around the curves of the inserts. Sew completely around the pieces, meeting up at the place you started.

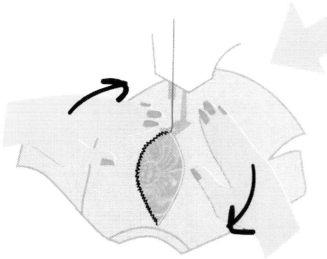

6. Finish sewing around all the inserts and cut any loose threads away.

7. Using embroidery scissors, cut away the T-shirt fabric that is covering the insert, making sure not to cut into the lace or into the zigzag stitches.

Your inserts are finished! Now your basic T-shirt is transformed into a sexy, glamorous design.

Using Sequins for a Sprinkle of Sparkle

Sequins are usually made from thin plastic, stamped in many different designs and colors from transparent to iridescent or with a mother-of-pearl coating. They are very easy to sew on by hand, using a small bead to anchor the sequin in place.

Sequins generally have one very tiny hole for sewing through and onto the fabric, so make sure the sewing needle is thin enough to go through the sequin hole. Use a beading needle or regular hand sewing needle, called sharp or between, size 10 with either embroidery thread or a silk, cotton, or all-purpose sewing thread, depending on the size of the sequin hole. Choose a thread color that matches the T-shirt or the sequin color. Sew on circular sequins with central holes one at a time, using one or two stitches to sew through the sequin hole. If you use two stitches, then they are sewn into the hole on opposite sides of the outer rim. Keep all the stitches facing in the same direction for a uniform look or vary the direction for a less formal look. You can also

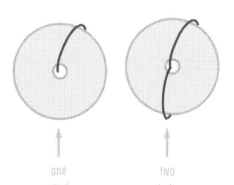

one
stitch

two
stitches

apply single hole sequins in rows by working a row of large backstitches and applying one sequin with each backstitch you sew.

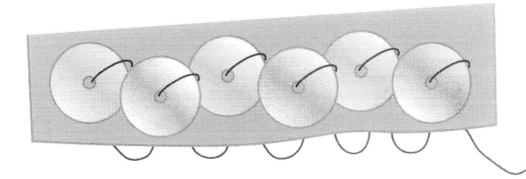

Rows of sequins can be bought by the yard and sewn on with clear sewing thread by machine using a zigzag stitch to go over the sequins. Make sure to set the zigzag stitch to a large enough width and length to go over the sequins. Use all-purpose thread in the bobbin of the sewing machine and clear nylon thread, if you desire, in the top threading of the machine. Try your T-shirt on and look in the mirror, then draw a nice design with a chalk line on the T-shirt. Follow this chalk line while sewing on the row of sequins. Take another piece of fabric, to test the zigzag stitch on your row of sequins. Try not to pierce the sequins and do not pull the sequins as you sew. By trying out the zigzag width and stitch length, you will get a feel of how to stitch down the row of sequins onto the fabric.

Cup sequins are round and dished in shape so they can not be sewn on the same way as flat sequins. With your hand-sewing needle, sew through the concave side of the sequin, then thread a tiny bead onto the needle and go back into the sequin hole. This will anchor the sequin in place. Some larger sequins or paillettes have slightly bigger holes. You can apply them with a single stitch through each hole in the paillette or bring the needle up through each hole and then sew on a cup sequin or a tiny bead for another effect.

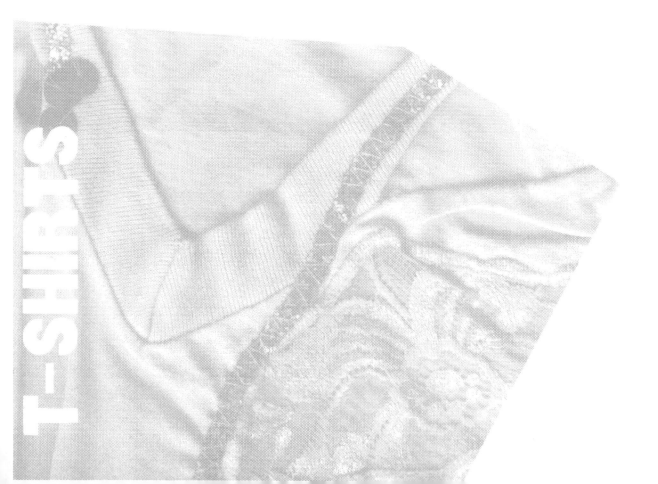

T-SHIRTS

Sewing in Decorative Zippers

Zippers can really add an interesting touch to T-shirts—and to all sorts of clothing. You can add zippers for functional purposes or for decorative purposes, as they were used on punk-style plaid pants in the 1970s.

One of my students sewed a white zipper onto the neckline of a plain old black crewneck sweater, and it made the sweater look trendy. I recommend metal zippers for this effect; however, any zipper will work—even one taken out of some of your old clothes. There are many different types of standard zippers made: nylon, plastic, metal, separating, two-way, and invisible. You can find some with rhinestones or shiny lurex on the zipper. Zipper teeth come in different sizes. Size 3 is small, 5 is medium, 7 is large, and 10 is extra large. (To give you a sense of the sizing, the zippers on jeans are usually small or medium; and the zippers on jackets are medium or large.)

For use on a T-shirt, go with a metal zipper with medium-size teeth. Try more than one zipper to make a real statement. Put on your T-shirt and stand in front of the mirror to decide on the placement of your zippers. With either straight pins or safety pins, pin your zippers to the places where you want to sew them. Then take the T-shirt off and lay it flat on a table. Make sure that you pin the zipper tape flat to the surface of the garment.

If you are sewing the zippers on by machine, it is really helpful to just take out your needle and thread to baste the zipper tape in place around the zipper. It is very easy to sew the zipper with the zipper tape exposed on top of any garment. You can use a straight stitch on your sewing machine, or test out some of the embroidery stitches to sew the zipper tape down. Always make sure to sew on the outside edges of the zipper tape. You can even go over the edge of the tape onto the fabric itself. If you are sewing the zipper by hand, use a backstitch to make it secure. You might even want to use a contrasting color thread to add a decorative effect on the zipper.

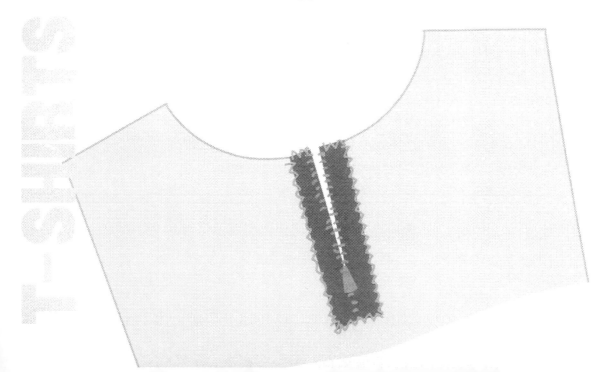

Turning an Old Baseball T-shirt into a Halter Top

Baseball T-shirts—or jerseys—with their distinctive look of a white body and colored raglan sleeves are seen everywhere. Though there are more stylized, fitted versions available for women, they're still too warm for a hot summer day. This summer heat-relief project can be done in less than an hour.

1. *Remove the neckline and sleeves by using a seam ripper. Carefully pick out the stitches to preserve the body of the shirt. Save the neck banding to use as the drawstring to hold the halter top around your neck.*

MATERIALS:

- baseball T-shirt
- seam ripper
- scissors
- straight pins
- thread to match your T-shirt
- sewing machine
- iron and ironing board
- needle if hand sewing
- ribbon

seam
ripper

2. At the top front and back of the remaining T-shirt body, chalk mark a 1-inch fold line. Fold this back to the wrong side and press with an iron. This will become the casing.

3. Insert the neck banding or a piece of ribbon of comparable length into the pressed casing. Then sew the casing either by hand using a backstitch or by machine, making sure not to sew through the inserted banding or ribbon.

4. Use the remaining neck banding to pull through the casing and tie around your neck on one side.

5. Now that you have a new halter top, add a heat-transfer picture (see opposite) or slogan to the front to really make it stand out.

Using Heat Transfers to Personalize Your T-Shirt

T-shirts with heat-transfer designs are sold everywhere, but making your own is easy to do, and instead of having to settle on what the store has to offer, you can have exactly what you want!

What you'll need to do this are a T-shirt, heat transfer paper, and an idea. To come up with ideas, surf the Web looking for images you like. Or use a design program on a computer to create an image all your own. If you're more interested in slogans—anything from something political ("Meat is murder") to something sassy ("Love means nothing")—all you need to do is type them up in the font you think looks best. You can get heat-transfer paper at superstores like Wal-Mart or Target and office-supply stores like Staples and Office Depot. Most kinds fit right into your printer, so you can print directly from your computer. Be sure to follow the directions carefully, as they vary a bit depending on what kind of printer and image you're working with. Once you have your printed image, follow the directions for transferring it onto your T-shirt, which should take a mere matter of minutes.

Also available and equally easy to use if you're creating a slogan shirt are iron-on letters, made out of felt, chenille yarn, fleece, or rhinestones. You can buy letters at fabric and crafts shops like Jo-Ann and Michaels.

Tips on Tinting and Dying Fabrics

Dying T-shirts is another way to transform an ordinary white shirt into a colorful, new-looking piece. It can also cover up stains that might have caused you to shelve a favorite old T-shirt.

The simplest way to do any dying is to use a brand of dye called Rit. It comes in liquid or powdered form and can be bought at any craft or art supply store and sometimes even in supermarkets. To use it, just follow the instructions on the packet or bottle. You can even use this dye in your washing machine, but after you've done your dying, be sure to run the washing machine through a complete cycle with soap.

Before you dye your item, you should wash it to get any dirt or dust off the T-shirt. To see if the intensity of the color you are using is dark or light enough, you should try a sample on a T-shirt or a scrap of fabric you do not need. Color always dries much lighter than it looks when it is wet.

If the color is too dark, you should add more water to the solution. If it is too light, you should add more dye. You can easily dye one T-shirt in a plastic bucket, bathtub, or big metal soup pot. Always wear rubber gloves or you will end up with colored hands.

Always submerge your T-shirt in plain hot water

before dropping it into the dye. After you have had the T-shirt submerged in the pot of dye for as long as the instructions say, do not forget to pour a tablespoon of coarse kitchen salt into the dye solution, which helps the dye retain its color.

USING COFFEE OR TEA TO TINT A T-SHIRT

MATERIALS

- at least 10 table-spoons of finely ground coffee or 4 teabags
- T-shirt or other article of white clothing
- large pot of water

1. *Brew a pot of coffee or tea.*

2. *Place the T-shirt in the pot of water to saturate the fabric.*

3. Add the boiled tea or coffee to the cold water and slowly bring it to a boil for a few minutes. Turn down the heat and let this mixture simmer for approximately half an hour and then pull the T-shirt out of the solution.

4. Squeeze out the remainder of the dye and lay the T-shirt down flat to dry. When it's dry it will have taken on a beautiful antique-beige glow.

CHAPTER 3

Sweatshirts

& Sweaters

fur-edged hoodie, see page 74

godets, see page 110

Sweatshirts and sweaters can be transformed into new styles very easily. This chapter will show you techniques on how to reconstruct, decorate, and trim.

Sweatshirts are made out of fleece, a knitted jersey fabric that is generally brushed on the wrong side. Around the 1930s, sweatshirts were made for athletes to wear while warming up or after sports. The earliest sweatshirts were utilitarian gray pullovers. In the late 1970s designer Norma Kamali started using sweatshirt material for women's fashions and turned a workaday fabric into a fashion statement. Today, sweatshirts with fleece letters and screen prints are worn by students on college campuses as well as hip-hop stars.

The movie *Flashdance* made the sweatshirt with the neckline cut off a hot look in the 1980s, and it's a look that continues to be popular today. But there are so many other simple ways to reinvent a drab sweatshirt into a new style. Even turning a sweatshirt inside out and using the wrong side as textural right side can be fun! Sweatshirts really can be as easy to reconstruct as T-shirts—in fact, you can use a lot of the same techniques explained in the T-shirt chapter on a sweatshirt! Like T-shirts, sweatshirt fabric or fleece won't fray, so you can cut into it and just leave the edges raw.

A Fast, Easy Sweatshirt Cardigan

I cut open one of my sweatshirts right through the logo on the front and then cut off the rib on the bottom and the sleeves, turning it into an instant cardigan. It amazed me how many compliments I got when it was so easy to do.

1. *Most sweatshirts are finished off with a ribbed knitted band around the neck, at the end of the sleeve, and the bottom of the body in order to allow for stretch. Start by cutting these off to give it a look that is less classically a sweatshirt.*

2. *Using your scissors, cut right along the sewn line where the rib was attached to the bottom of the sweatshirt and end of the sleeves.*

3. *Fold the front of the sweatshirt in half. Be careful to make sure that the sweatshirt is folded exactly in half by matching the shoulder lines of the sweatshirt together as well as the side seams. Then pin them so that the front is evenly folded in half.*

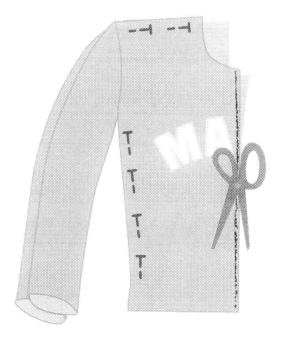

4. *Chalk mark the center-front fold of the sweatshirt from the top of the neckline to the bottom of the sweatshirt. Take your scissors and cut open the front of the sweatshirt by following the chalk mark drawn down the center front. It's that easy!*

You can also cut the sleeves out of the new sweatshirt cardigan that you've made and turn it into a vest. This is very easily done with your seam ripper by carefully cutting the stitching open all around the armholes of the sweatshirt. Or you might want to add sleeves from a different jacket, like an army-surplus jacket.

Then, if you're still not done, there are plenty of other embellishments that can be added. Hand tack on chains, charms, or add some bling by arranging some glitzy buttons in a cluster to look like a trendy brooch. Vivienne Westwood even used boiled chicken bones and chains on an old sweatshirt. Ribbons are a great decoration. Use a straight stitch or zigzag stitch to attach them. Be careful about sewing ribbons on the diagonal or bias— it may cause the sweatshirt to bubble, but that might look funky anyway. You can also use stamps and colorfast ink to stamp a design pattern.

Adding Fake Fur Trim to a Hoodie

MATERIALS

- ½ yard of fake fur
- cotton hoodie
- straight pins
- marking chalk or pencil
- tape measure
- scissors
- fabric glue
- all-purpose thread to match the fur if machine sewing
- sewing machine
- darning needle if hand sewing
- 100-percent polyester thread or button and carpet thread to match the fur if sewing by hand

Fake fur comes in so many varieties and thickness or pile which is the length of the fur hair. Some furs are easier to handle than others. You might even have fur trim on an old coat or jacket that can be removed and used for this project. Always cut the fake fur with the wrong side facing you. When cutting out fur, be prepared for a lot of lint and fur flying around. When sewing fur trim by machine, set the stitch length to the longest length. Also, use a size-14 jeans needle. If sewing by hand, use a longer, thicker needle called a darner.

ADDITIONAL TIPS ON SEWING REAL FUR TRIM—*Real fur can be cut like fake fur. With a single-edge razor blade, you can shave away some of the fur on the seam allowance in order to make it easier to sew. Sewing through the leather back of the fur by hand can be tough, so use a needle-nose pliers to help pull a leather needle through the fur. Also use either 100-percent polyester thread or button and carpet thread.*

1. *Cut off the ribbed band or finished hem on the sleeves. Lay hood on a table folded in half. Using a tape measure, measure half the hood lengthwise, starting at the top and ending at the neckline. Then measure around the end of a sleeve. Double the hood measurement, plus double the end-of-sleeve measurement, plus 1-inch for seam allowance on each cuff is the length of fur you'll need, by 3 inches wide. For example, if the hood measures 27 inches and cuffs are 24 inches, then the total length of the fur will be 51 inches long by 3 inches wide.*

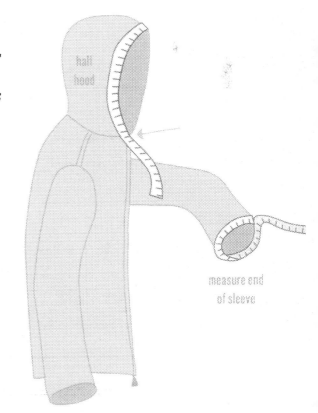

half hood

measure end of sleeve

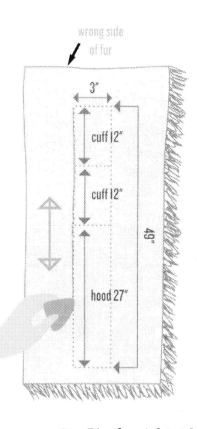

wrong side
of fur

3"

cuff 12"

cuff 12"

hood 27"

49"

2. *On the back side of the fur, chalk out the total length, width, and cut lines for the hood and each cuff. This is the 27-inch line for hood, 12-inches and 12-inches for two cuffs. Cut out each section using very sharp scissors. Take small snips with the tips of your scissors, pushing the fur hair out of the way.*

3. *Pin the right side of the fur 1-inch in toward the inside edge of the hood. Sew this onto the hood either by hand or machine. Bend the fur back toward the right side of the hood.*

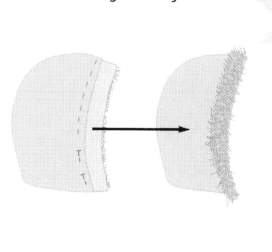

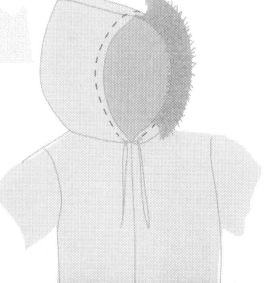

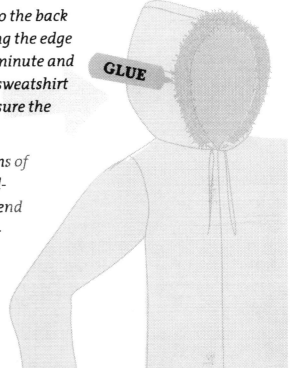

GLUE

4. Using fabric glue, apply the glue to the back of the fur along the edge and along the edge of the hood. Let the glue set for a minute and then press the fur down onto the sweatshirt holding it with pressure to make sure the glue sticks.

5. Sew together the 3-inch wide seams of the fur cuffs using ½-inch seam allowance. Insert the cuffs into the end of the sleeve, with the fur side facing the right side of the sleeve. Match the seam allowance of the fur with the seam allowance of the sleeve.

6. To attach the fur cuff to the sleeve, sew around the opening on the wrong side of the fur, using ½-inch seam allowance. If your sewing machine has a free arm, remove it to help you sew around the sleeve opening. Turn the fur onto the right side, and you have an upbeat hoodie to wear.

Making a Simple Appliqué Design Your Sweatshirt

An appliqué is a design made out of one or more different fabrics and then sewn onto another fabric or garment. This technique can create texture and add interest to a sweatshirt. You can also use it in many other places on clothing such as pants or skirts, or home decor, such as on pillows. You can sew an appliqué either by machine or by hand, or use both as part of the appliqué design.

For example, a butterfly composed of several different fabrics will look great as an appliqué. You can even cut out different parts of printed fabrics, such as cutting out the flowers from a floral-printed fabric and leaves from another printed fabric, combining them together to form your appliqué design. Appliqués can also be created out of parts of old jeans or pockets from jackets and pants.

Collect scraps of different kinds of fabrics. Using a varied assortment of fabrics in your appliqué can add interesting texture to the design. Fabrics can be prints, plaids, stripes, or solids. They can be woven or knitted, felt, and even fur or leather. Also consider the texture of velvet, suede, and metallics. Anything goes when making an interesting appliqué piece. Keep in mind that you will need a little experience to work with leather, suede, or fur pieces.

1. *Draw out the design on paper or trace it from a picture using tracing paper or vellum. A simple design is always best if you are new at this. Choose the fabrics that you will use in each layer of the design, and keep in mind that it's best to have no more than three layers to the appliqué. Otherwise, it can be hard to sew through all the thickness.*

MATERIALS

- small pieces of fabric for your design
- straight pins
- scissors
- vellum, tracing paper, or Wonder Under fusible web
- fusible mending tape (if you are not using Wonder Under)
- all-purpose thread to match or contrast with your fabric
- sewing machine
- iron and ironing board
- embroidery needle if hand sewing

2. *Pin your pattern pieces onto each different fabric and cut them out.*

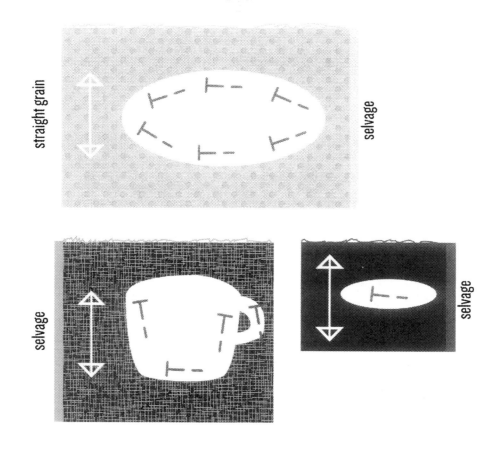

3. *To secure the appliqué design onto the garment, use an iron-on fuse tape. Take small bits of fuse tape and slip them in between the appliqué piece and the garment. Steam press the appliqué piece. Start with the bottom layer of your design and fuse it. Then add the next layer on top and fuse it down. Con-*

tinue this process for all the layers of the appliqué until your design is glued onto the garment. This will make it easy to handle while sewing it. (Another easy way to make appliqué designs is by using a product called Wonder Under. It's like fuse tape, but you can draw your design right onto it and iron the appliqué onto your garment in three easy steps by following the instructions on the package.)

4. If you are sewing by machine, first test out the zigzag stitch to make sure that the stitch width is covering the edge of the appliqué and that the machine doesn't jam by having the stitches too close together. The zigzag stitch is usually best when it's the widest. The stitch length should be set on 2 or 3. The smaller the stitch the more the threads will cover the raw edges of the appliqué since the stitches will pack up closer together.

Sew down the first layer of the appliqué and continue to sew around the other layers of the appliqué until they are all sewn down. Also consider using another contrasting color of sewing thread for the zigzag stitch. It may add interesting dimension to the appliqué design. For an extra touch, try hand sewing some beads or sequins here and there on the appliqué.

Quick Techno Appliqué

This technique combines your computer skills and sewing skills to make an arty appliqué on a sweatshirt.

MATERIALS

- sweatshirt
- heat-transfer paper that is made for printing on dark colors
- all-purpose thread if machine sewing
- sewing machine
- iron and ironing board
- embroidery needle if hand sewing
- embroidery thread if hand sewing

1. *Print your own designs onto heat-transfer paper with your computer. Make them small sizes, measuring approximately 3-inches square or 3 by 4 inches. Arrange the patches on the sweatshirt to form a design you like, then iron them onto the sweatshirt.*

2. *Using either some machine decorative stitches or hand-embroidery stitches, sew around the iron-on patches to create a picture frame effect.*

Turn Two Old Sweatshirts into a Wrap Sweatshirt

MATERIALS

- two old sweatshirts that are the same size
- straight pins
- marking chalk or pencil
- clear ruler
- Wonder Under fusible web
- all-purpose thread to match your fabric
- sewing machine

1. *With a scissors, cut away the whole front of one of the sweatshirts. Begin by cutting the front right alongside the sewn seam lines. Save the back piece for cutting out the ties. Then cut off the ribbed band on the bottom. Lay this front on a table with the right side facing you and chalk mark a cutting line. Start from where the neckline meets the shoulder line and draw a cutting line down the front. Make sure the cutting line extends to the left of the center front. Cut apart the front on the cutting line and throw the remaining piece away.*

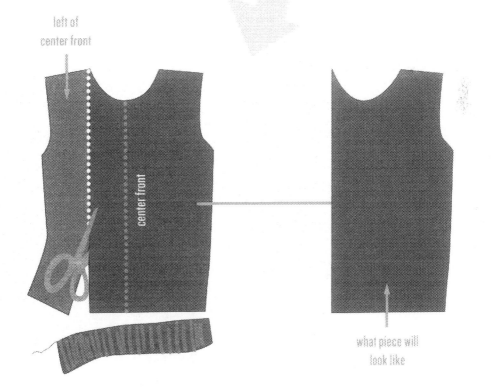

left of
center front

center front

what piece will
look like

2. *Cut off the rib trim on the sleeves and the bottom of the second sweatshirt. Lay this sweatshirt on a table with the front right side facing you. Start from where the neckline meets the shoulder line. Draw a cutting line down the front, making sure the cutting line extends to the right of the center front.*

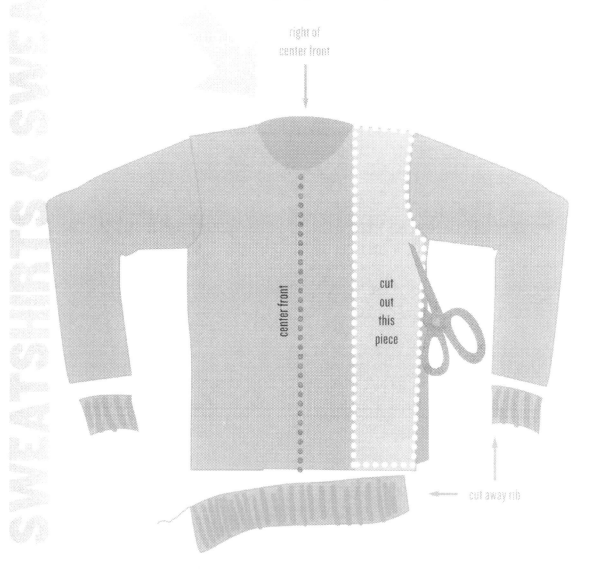

right of center front

center front

cut out this piece

cut away rib

3. Cut apart the front on this cutting line and then continue to cut the remaining part of the front away at the shoulder seam around the front of the armhole and down the side seam. Throw this part away.

4. Pin the cut-out sweatshirt front onto the body of the second sweatshirt by starting at the cut away shoulder. Pin around the armhole, attaching the armhole to the half-opened sleeve, and down the side seam. Now you should have two fronts that wrap.

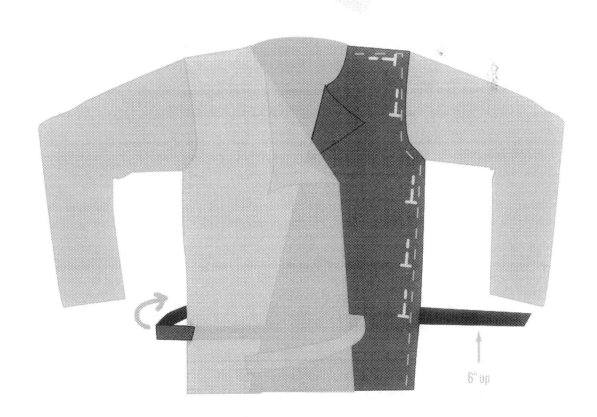

6" up

5. *Sew the new side into the sweatshirt either on the wrong side or right side.*

6. *Use the leftover back of the first sweatshirt to make the ties. Chalk mark a 1½-inches wide by 27-inches long tie and another 1½-inches wide by 12 inches long tie. For the 27-inch-long tie, you might have to piece it together using two cut lengths of the remaining sweatshirt. On the left side seam of your sweatshirt, measure up from the bottom approximately 6 inches and cut open a 1-inch hole to pull your tie through.*

7. *Sew the 27-inch long tie 6 inches up to the underside of the wrap and then sew on the 12-inch-long tie 6 inches up on the side front that wraps over in the front. For a real snug fit along the side seams and sleeves, do a fitting, using the fitting instructions on pages 38 to 40 and take in the sweatshirt.*

You now have the coolest, wrap sweatshirt around!

SWEATERS

The knitting of sweaters has gone on for centuries, so naturally there have been a bazillion kinds of sweaters knitted and crocheted in all sorts of different patterns, from cables and ribs and in all kinds of yarns from tweeds to bouclés. Depending on the size of the yarn, sweaters can be anything from bulky to very flat and thin in appearance. Some sweaters have a ribbed finish at the bottom of the body of the sweater, end of the sleeve, and neckline, which is designed to give extra stretch to those areas.

rib

Mix and Match

Got any old sweaters buried in your dresser drawers? Pull them out, because here's an opportunity to experiment, chop them up, and reinvent them into a new one. You can create a new sweater from old sweaters by cutting apart sections of the fronts, backs, and sleeves and swapping the pieces to make a completely different sweater of rearranged colors and patterns. (Save any pieces you cut for use as accessories, which you'll read about in chapter 6.)

For the next two projects, you'll need at least three sweaters you don't mind cutting up. (For the second project, one of them will need to be a turtleneck.) The colors should look good together, and try to find sweaters that are knitted of approximately the same thickness yarn (for example, if you have a sweater that is almost like a T-shirt knit it won't look good combined with a very chunky knit). Examine them to see if they have any holes or tears—you might not want the hole or tear included in the new design, or you might want to feature it in some original way.

Hand sewing with yarn can also be used as a form of decoration over the machine stitches. These projects can be sewn together either on the wrong or right side of the sweater, depending on the look you want.

BICOLORED AT SLEEVE AND BOTTOM

1. *Choose one sweater to be the body of the newly designed sweater, and use the others for pieces.*

2. *On the sweater body you've chosen, measure up from the bottom 3½ inches and cut off evenly all around the bottom of the sweater. On one of the other sweaters, measure up from the bottom 4½ inches all around and cut an evenly measured bottom off of that sweater.*

MATERIALS FOR THE NEXT TWO PROJECTS

- for each project, at least three old sweaters; for the second project, one sweater should be a turtleneck
- straight pins
- marking chalk or pencil
- tape measure or clear ruler
- dressmaker's scissors
- seam ripper
- all-purpose thread
- sewing machine
- tapestry needle if hand sewing
- fingering-weight yarn, baby yarn, or tapestry yarn if hand sewing

sweater body

3½"

other sweater

4½"

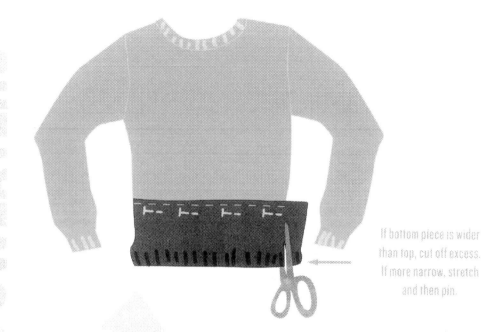

If bottom piece is wider than top, cut off excess. If more narrow, stretch and then pin.

3. Pin the 4½-inch bottom onto the cut bottom of the new sweater body, either with wrong sides or the right sides together, depending on the reconstructed look you want. If the sweaters are different in size, cut down or stretch the 4½-inch bottom to fit the circumference of the sweater body you are attaching it to. Carefully pin and sew the bottom onto the new sweater body, using ½-inch seam allowance.

4. *On the new sweater body sleeves, measure up 11 inches from the bottom of the sleeves and cut off the bottom part of the sleeves. On one of the other old sweaters measure up 12 inches from the bottom of the sleeves and cut them off too.*

5. *Pin the cut-off old sleeves onto the cut-off sleeves of the sweater body, and then sew them together, using ½-inch seam allowance.*

A BICOLOR TURTLENECK

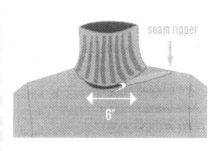

seam ripper

6"

1. *With your seam ripper, pick open approximately 6 inches of the center-front neckline area.*

2. *Fold the turtleneck in half and pin the shoulders and the side seams together. Chalk mark the center-front fold of your turtleneck sweater from the neckline down to the bottom of the sweater.*

3. *Measure in from the center fold of the sweater 1½-inches and chalk mark a line from the neckline to the bottom of the sweater. Using a scissors, cut out this piece of the sweater. It will serve as the pattern piece for the vertical insert you'll cut from one of the other sweaters.*

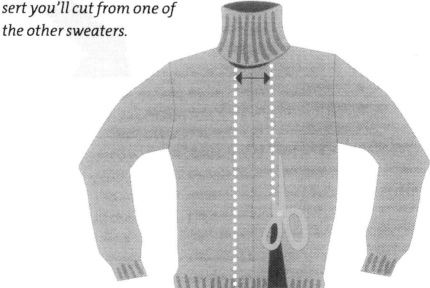

4. *Choose the sweater that you think will look good as the vertical insert and pin the pattern piece onto it. Chalk mark an extra 1-inch seam allowance to the pattern on all sides except the bottom and then cut it out.*

5. *Insert this new piece into the front of the sweater body and pin in place. Sew the two lengthwise seams, using ½-inch seam allowance.*

6. *At the center front, sew turtleneck back onto the newly inserted piece. Save your leftover sweater scraps. They can be used as an appliqué decoration on another sweater, or even on the tote bag I'll show you how to make later on in this chapter.*

1" wider than the strip from other sweater

Create a Shrug Out of a Button-Front Cardigan Sweater

MATERIALS

- button-front cardigan sweater
- straight pins
- marking chalk or pencil
- Scotch tape or ¼-inch masking tape
- scissors
- all-purpose thread
- sewing machine
- tapestry needle if hand sewing
- fingering-weight yarn, baby yarn, or tapestry yarn if hand sewing

1. Stand in front of the mirror and try on your sweater to decide where you want to cut it off for a shrug style.

2. With Scotch tape or ¼-inch masking tape, mark the new style line on one side of the cardigan for your shrug.

3. *Fold the cardigan in half. Make sure that the cardigan is folded exactly in half by matching the shoulder lines together as well as the side seams. Then pin them together.*

4. *Cut off the length of the cardigan, following the taped style line and continue to the center back of the sweater.*

5. *Pin the leftover rib trim from the cardigan (or from another sweater) around the new style line to give the shrug a finished look. Make sure you have enough rib to go all the way around the shrug. Start pinning the rib on at the neckline on one side of the new front and continue all around the back to the other side. You can overlap the rib onto the edge of the shrug approximately ½ inch and then use a zigzag or another decorative stitch, by hand or machine, to sew on the rib.*

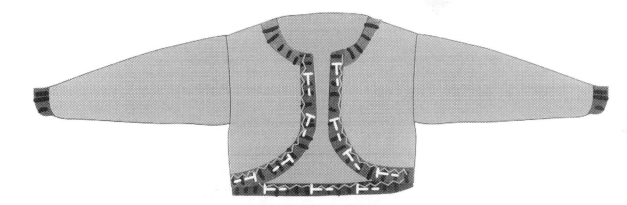

Sweater Tote

Transforming an old sweater into a simple tote is easy to do using a single sweater or pieces patched together from a couple of old chunky knitted sweaters. (Even combining other fabrics, such as fake fur or corduroy with the leftover knit will make unusual bags.) These easy instructions will get you going on your first tote.

This bag will be much stronger if sewn by machine, but if you are sewing this by hand, use a darning needle and all-purpose thread or button and carpet thread.

MATERIALS

- chunky-knit pullover sweater
- ½ yard of iron-on fusible interfacing
- straight pins
- marking chalk or pencil
- clear ruler
- scissors
- seam ripper
- all-purpose thread to match the sweater color
- sewing machine
- iron and ironing board
- darning needle if hand sewing
- all-purpose or button and carpet thread if hand sewing
- fuse tape

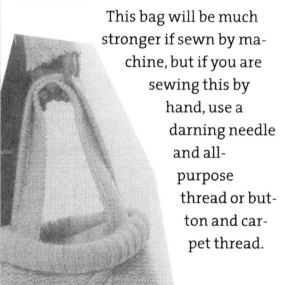

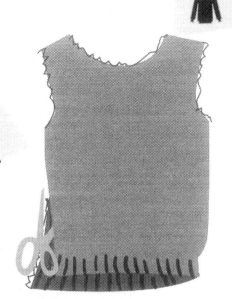

1. *Separate the front and back of the sweater by cutting open the side seams. Then cut open the armhole seams and remove the sleeves. Cut open the shoulder seams and continue by cutting through the neckline. Cut open the two sleeves at the underarm seams.*

2. *Lay your front and back pieces on a table and with the clear ruler, chalk mark out two rectangles 13 inches wide at the bottom, 12 inches wide at the top, and 14 inches long. These measurements include a 1-inch bend back at the top and ½-inch seam allowance on the other three sides of the tote. If the sweater you are using is too small for the dimensions given, you can scale down the size of the tote to fit the size sweater you have.*

3. *Cut out the tote along the chalk line. Cut the fusible interfacing using the same measurements as the tote.*

12"

14"

13"

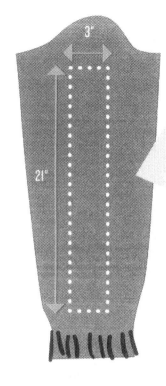

4. *Using the two sleeves, cut straps for the tote, 3 inches wide by 21 inches long. Cut the fusible interfacing the same size as the straps.*

5. *Use the steam setting on your iron to press the fusible to the wrong side of the cut sweater squares and the wrong side of the sleeve straps. Make sure that the glue side of the fusible is facing down toward the sweater. Hold the steam iron on the fusible for at least one minute to make sure the fusible interfacing is sticking to the sweater. After fusing the straps, fold them in half with the wrong sides together and the raw edges showing deliberately.*

6. Set the stitch length on your sewing machine to the largest stitch, and sew the bag using a ½-inch seam allowance on all three sides.

7. Turn your tote right side out. In order to pull the corners out so they lay flat, take the point of your scissors and push gently inside the bag at each corner to make a crisp point. Press the seams flat using a steam iron.

8. Bend the top of the bag 1 inch toward the inside. Insert fuse tape in between the 1-inch fold back and the bag. Steam press all around the top of the bag, making sure the fuse tape is gluing the two sides together.

9. Sew the length of the straps together, ⅛ inch away from the raw edges. Then pin the ends of the straps onto the inside of the bag 2 inches down from the top. Space each end of the straps approximately 7 inches apart. Sew over each strap back and forth at least two times.

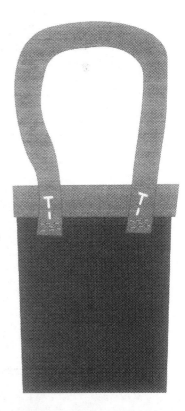

CHAPTER 4

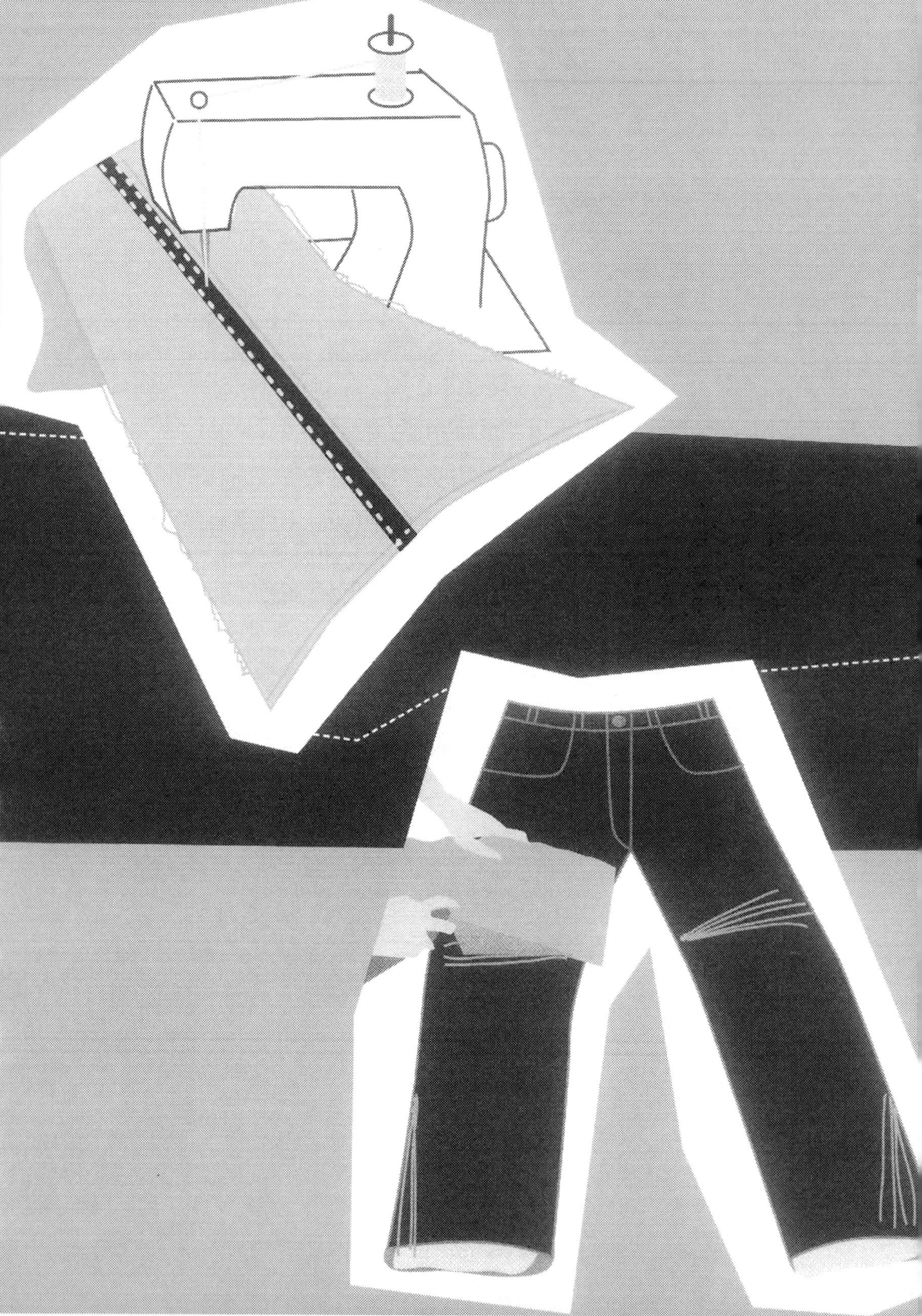

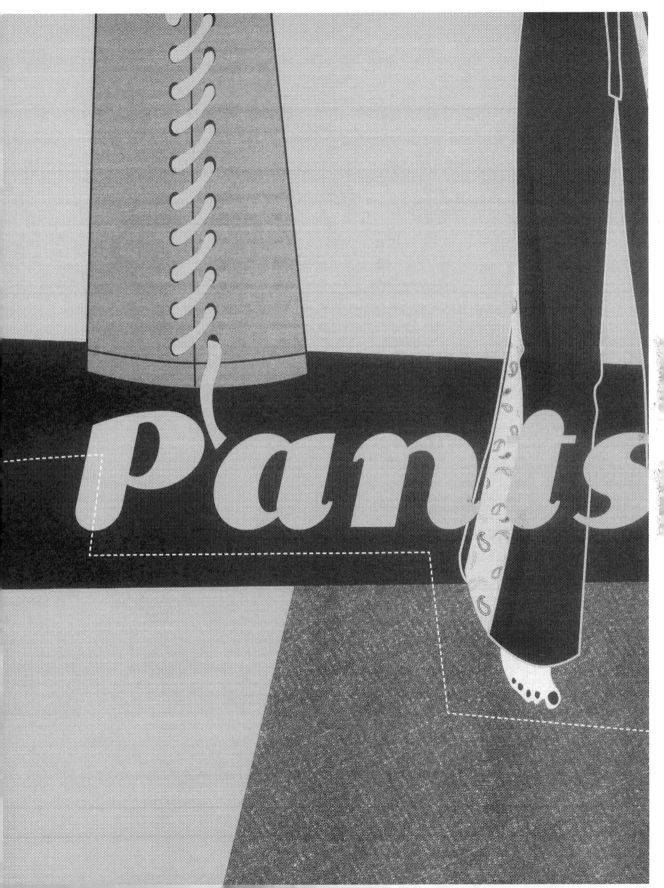

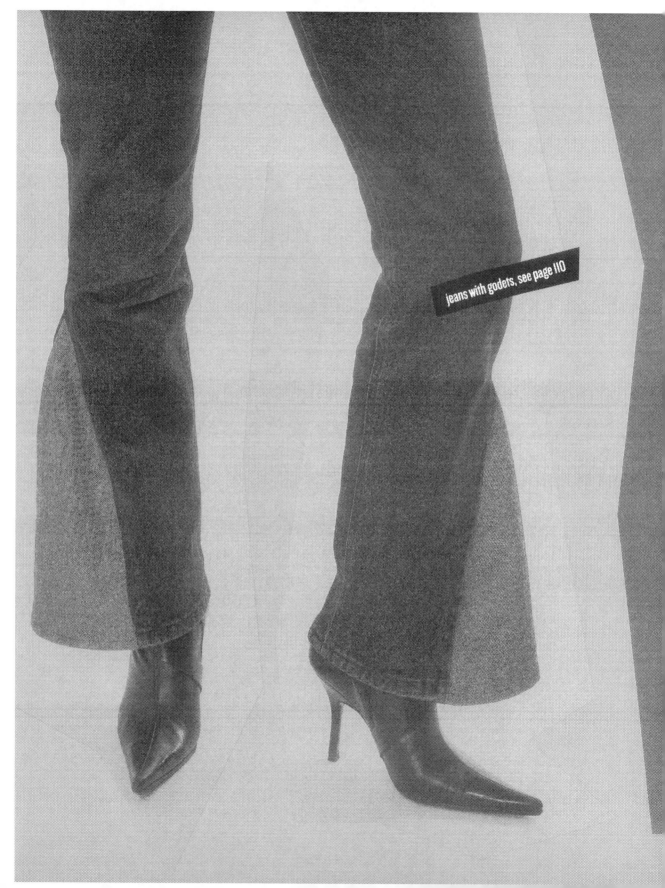
jeans with godets, see page 110

There are many changes you can make to your pants, trousers, and jeans to turn them into a new style. Depending on the fashion trends of the season, pants go through dramatic changes, from high waist to way below the belly button, wide leg to pencil thin, cropped to the shortest shorts. With a few basic projects under your belt, you'll be able to keep up with all the trends—sometimes with the same pair of pants!

Chop off your khakis into cropped pants or Bermuda shorts. Take a pair of trousers and renew them with satin ribbon down the side seams to give them the look of tuxedo pants. Give your jeans a deliberate worn look by bleaching them and cutting slashes in places like the knees, or cut off the waistband and belt loops for a raw look. Add some lacings on the side seams of your pants. All these techniques, as well as others, are covered in this chapter. So last season's pants with just a simple redo can become this season's favorite to wear.

Add a Tuxedo Stripe to Your Trousers

- trousers
- 2½ yards of satin ribbon, preferably ⅞ of an inch wide
- straight pins
- scissors
- seam ripper
- all-purpose thread to match the ribbon
- sewing machine
- iron and ironing board
- sharp or between needle if hand sewing

If you find an old pair of pleated trousers or men's pants at the thrift store or hanging in a yard sale, you can easily transform them into a fashionable tuxedo look just by adding satin ribbon down the side seams.

1. Lay your trousers down with the side seam of the pant facing you, one pant leg on top of the other.

2. For ribbon length, measure the finished trouser length, and add 1 inch for folding in the raw edges of the ribbon on the top and the bottom of the trouser. Double this measurement for both pant legs, then cut the ribbon in half.

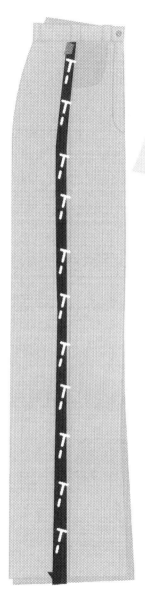

3. Place the ribbon directly under the waistband and bend in ½ inch on the end of the ribbon toward the wrong side. Pin the ribbon onto the pant leg with the edge resting on the back side of the side seam of the pant. At the bottom of the pant leg, again turn ½ inch of ribbon under to have a clean edge. Do this on both side seams.

4. In order to sew the ribbon onto the side seams by machine, you might have to open the inseam of the pant part of the way. Using a seam ripper start 4 inches up from the bottom leg and open the inseam approximately 18 inches.

5. *Place the pant leg into the sewing machine. If your sewing machine has a free arm, remove it since it will make it easier to sew the ribbon down the pant legs. Start at the top under the waistband to sew one edge of the ribbon down to the bottom of the pant and then sew the other edge of the ribbon down to the bottom of the pant. Now sew the inseams closed and press the pant legs on an ironing board.*

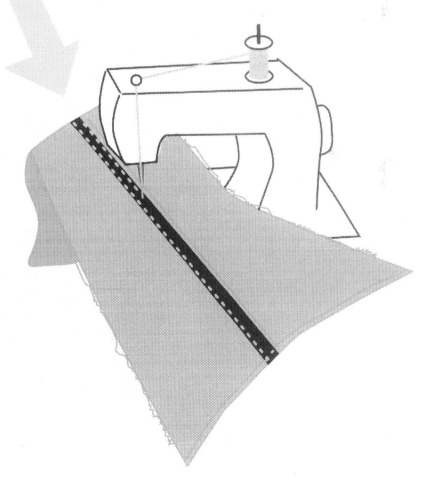

MATERIALS

- jeans
- ½ yard of fabric or leftover pant legs for the godet
- paper for your godet pattern
- straight pins
- marking chalk or pencil
- clear ruler
- scissors
- seam ripper
- all-purpose thread
- sewing machine
- iron and ironing board
- darning needle if hand sewing

Turn Straight Legs into Bell Bottoms

Godets are inserts shaped like wedges of a pie that will add a little flare to skirts or pants and look especially great added to jeans.

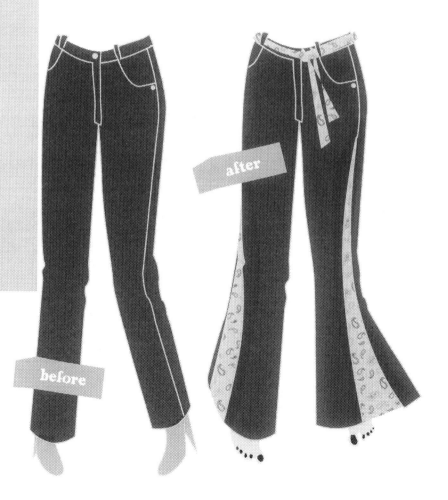

before

after

1. *Put on your jeans and go to the mirror to determine where you want the top of your godet to start. Use a pencil or marking chalk to cross mark this placement. Then take the jeans off and with a seam ripper start to pick open the side seams. For a very long godet, start it from your full hipline. Using a seam ripper, cut through the overlock stitch or the felled seam on the inside of the jeans. (An overlock stitch overcasts and finishes the seams so they don't fray, and a felled seam also finishes a seam with a double stitch.)*

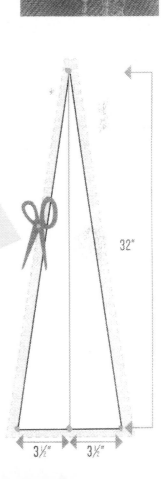

felled seam   overlock stitch

inside side seam of jeans

2. *To make the godet pattern, mark the measurement from the point that you marked on side seam to the bottom hem of the jean on a piece of paper. This becomes the length of your godet pattern. For example, 32 inches long is the lengthwise grain of the godet.*

3. *Draw a horizontal line perpendicular to 32-inch lengthwise grain. Measure how wide you want the godet and divide it in half. For example, a 7-inch wide godet divided in half is 3½ inches. Mark this on each side of the perpendicular line. Connect the points to form a triangle. Add an extra ½ inch all around the triangle for seam allowance, then cut out the paper pattern.*

32"

3½"   3½"

4. *Pin your godet pattern onto the fabric. Make sure to pin the pattern on the lengthwise grain of your fabric. For instance, when using a leftover pant leg from another pair of blue jeans, the lengthwise grain is running vertically along the leg of the pant. Fold the fabric in half in order to cut the two godets at the same time. Pin pattern through both layers of fabric and then cut it out.*

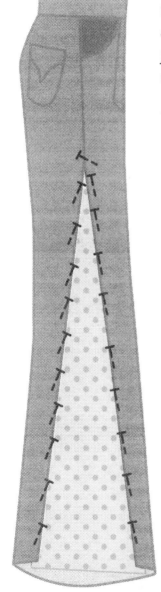

5. *Pin the right side of the godet to the right side of the blue jean leg. Start by pinning the point of the godet into the top of the opening of the jean. Then pin the rest of the godet into the opened side seams. Make sure to leave an extra inch on the bottom of the godet for a hem.*

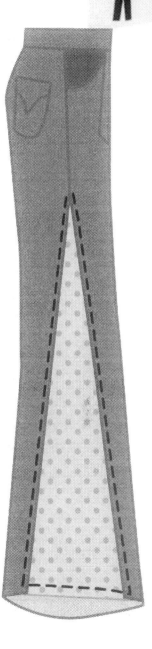

6. *Baste the side seams of the jean to the godet, starting from the bottom working toward the point. Start sewing from the bottom up to the point on both sides of the godet. At the bottom of the godet, bend up the extra 1 inch toward the wrong side in order to create the hem and bend in the raw edge for a clean hemline. Sew the hemline of the godet, or leave a raw edge, but remember to then cut off the extra 1-inch seam allowance of the godet.*

7. *Press the seams open and the godet point flat.*

Turn Khaki Pants into Cropped Pants or Bermuda Shorts

It's really easy to update an old pair of pants and give them a new life just by making them into crop pants or Bermuda shorts.

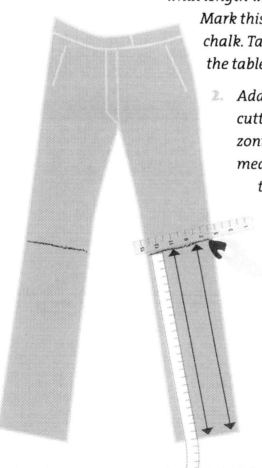

1. *Try on the pants in front of the mirror to determine what length will be best for your cropped pants. Mark this length with safety pins or marking chalk. Take off your pants and lay them flat on the table.*

2. *Add 1 inch for the hem and then mark a cutting line with chalk and a ruler horizontally across the pant leg. Do this by measuring up from the original length of the pants across the front.*

MATERIALS

- khakis
- safety pins
- marking chalk or pencil
- clear ruler
- scissors

3.   To cut both legs evenly, fold the marked pant leg directly on top of the other pant leg, making sure to match the side seams and inseams. Pin the legs together, keeping them flat on a table so that both legs can be cut off evenly at the same time.

4.   At the new cut hemline, bend up the pant legs 1 inch toward the wrong side of the pants. Now turn in ¼ inch at the raw edge so that the hemline has a clean finish. Press the hem in place on an ironing board, then sew the hem close to the edge using a sewing machine or use a blind hemstitch by hand.

- **all-purpose thread to match your fabric**
- **sewing machine**
- **iron and ironing board**
- **sharp or between needle if hand sewing**

Adding Lacing to the Side Seams of Jeans

MATERIALS

- jeans
- lacing material such as shoelaces, thin cording, leather cord, or ribbon
- marking chalk or pencil
- clear ruler or tape measure
- embroidery scissors
- seam ripper
- awl
- optional: Dritz eyelet kit. Follow instructions included.

Like lace-up boots, adding crisscross lacing to the side seams of jeans makes for a very different look.

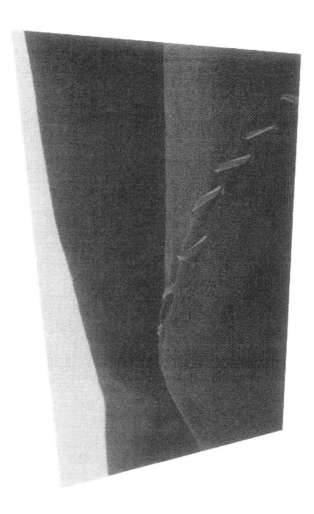

1. *To mark the lacing holes, lay your jeans on the table with the side seams facing you. Use a pencil to mark the center of each hole and make sure to have the same amount of holes on each side of the garment. Space them at least 1½ inches apart on each side. Start the lacing no higher than 18 inches up from the bottom opening of the leg. You might have to open the inseam in order to be able to make the holes and do the lacing. Use a seam ripper to open but don't open up the inseam any higher than 25 inches.*

2. *Use the tips of your scissors or an awl to cut into the mark for each lacing hole. The hole should not be more than a ½ inch wide.*

3. *Knot the end of your lacing in order to keep it from pulling through. Starting at the top, thread the lacing in, starting from the wrong side of your jeans and pulling the lacing out to the right side. Continue lacing to the bottom of the side seams of your jeans. End your lacing with a slipknot either on the wrong or right side, depending on what looks best to you.*

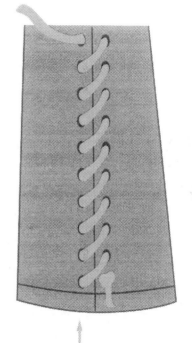

pant
hem

Adding Patches

- jeans
- various fabric scraps
- safety pins
- scissors
- fusible hem tape or Wonder Under fusible web
- all-purpose thread
- sewing machine
- Teflon presser foot and size-14 machine needle if sewing leather
- iron and ironing board
- darning needle if hand sewing

Fabric patches look very interesting on pants or jeans, so give your pants a real customized look by designing your own patches in any size or shape. They can be cut out from left-over parts of jeans or pants, shirts, in fabrics such as cottons, twills, corduroy, leather, suede, or vinyl.

When sewing leather, suede, or vinyl by machine, change your all-purpose foot to a Teflon foot and also change the needle in your sewing machine to a size-14 jeans needle. If sewing by hand, use a leather needle, button and carpet thread or 100 percent polyester thread. You might have to use a needle-nose pliers to help pull the needle through. For fabric, use a darning needle.

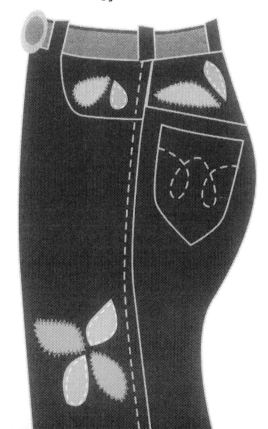

1. *Cut out your patches to any size or shape. The raw edges of the fabric can be left as they are or pressed under toward the wrong side for a more finished look.*

2. *Arrange them on the pant leg in different places to see if you like how they look. Once you've moved them around several different ways to decide what looks best, pin them onto the pants.*

3. *A fast way to attach patches permanently is by using iron-on fusible mending tape. Tear pieces of the fuse tape and insert them in between the patches and the pant. With a good steam iron, steam them down onto the pants. Check to see if the fuse tape has melted by picking up the patch a little. If not, hold the steam iron down on the patches for a longer time. (Another product that makes ironing on patches easy to do is Wonder Under, which is similar to fuse tape.)*

4. *If you are sewing patches onto a slim-fitting jean or pant by machine, you might have to open either the inseams or outseams part way in order to insert them into the sewing machine. Use a seam ripper to open the seams, but don't open the bottom end of the pants.*

5. *Sewing on and over the patches will also add to the decorative effect. Use a straight stitch in contrasting or matching thread, but make the stitch length as long as possible. Experiment and try some decorative stitches such as a zigzag stitch.*

Give Jeans a Bleached and Worn-Out Look

Jeans come in absolutely every shade of blue now, and it can be fun to experiment with your existing jeans to get them to the exact shade you want. Bleaching jeans is mostly experimental until you get the right amount of fading. There are several ways to achieve the bleached-out and worn look. One of the most basic ways is to put your jeans in the washing machine, and use hot water, detergent, and approximately three cups of bleach. If you want the jeans to be lighter, keep adding more bleach. There are also products made especially to create a faded blue jean. One is Dylon Easy Bleach, which is available at most fabric stores, as is Fast Fade by Rit. To overdye, use a package of Rit tan powder dye.

There a few effective ways to create a worn look in the texture of the jeans. One is to use fine-grade sandpaper and rub on the areas where you want your jeans to look faded. The sandpaper wears down the threads in the denim. You can also achieve this with a citrus rind grater by rubbing it briskly over the area of the jean where you want this effect. Another technique to make jeans soft and generally worn looking is to put them in the dryer for about half an hour with some tennis balls.

Adding Whiskers to Jeans

One of my students learned to paint jeans with light stripes that look like crease lines to give his jeans a new kind of distressed look. To do this, all you need is a regular can of silver spray paint that you can get in a hardware store like Home Depot. This is a great outdoor project to do on a sunny, dry day, but if you do it inside, be sure to work in a well-ventilated room.

MATERIALS

- jeans
- silver spray paint
- newspaper
- rectangular piece of cardboard from a carton or box

1. *Make sure to cover the floor and nearby areas with newspaper.*

2. *Stuff the legs of the jeans with some newspaper so that the spray paint won't saturate through to the other side of the jeans. Lay the front of the jeans down flat and facing you.*

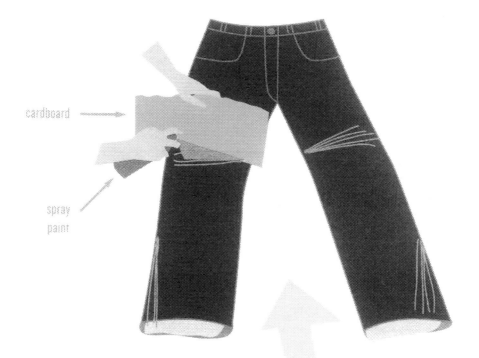

cardboard

spray
paint

3. *Very lightly spray streaks onto the front of the jeans, but be careful not to get the paint too concentrated. To control the streaks, hold a piece of cardboard just on top of the area of the jeans where you plan to spray the paint streaks. Use the cardboard as a guide for the streak line while spraying the can of paint. Be careful not to spay too much in one place, otherwise the paint will become too saturated. In order to get comfortable with this technique, practice using the paint on a test piece of fabric.*

How to Shorten Your Jeans without Losing the Original Hem

Want your jeans to be shorter, but don't want to lose the original faded and worn out hem? This technique has been proven to fool the eye.

1. *Put your jeans on and stand in front of the mirror to decide how much you need to shorten. Turn the bottom of one leg up toward the outside of the leg until you've reached the desired length and then put two pins just under the original sewn hem.*

2. *Take off your jeans and lay them on the table with the pinned pant leg on top. Fold up the second leg making sure it matches the length of the pinned one. With your ruler, evenly measure the same amount you pinned up all around on each leg.*

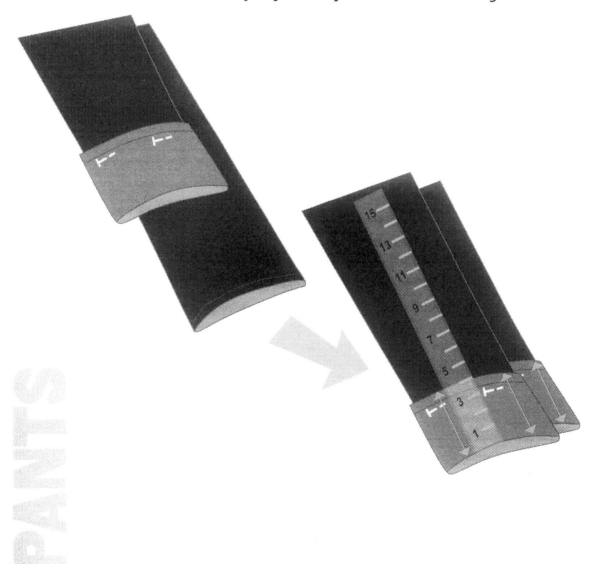

3. Change the all-purpose foot on your sewing machine to a zipper foot. With the zipper foot placed very close to the edge of the of the original hem sew around, following the edge of the original jean hem on the wrong side.

4. Push the excess up toward the inside of the jean leg and then press firmly on an ironing board. If the excess is more than 1 inch then cut some away making sure to leave at least ⅝ inch. Change back to your all-purpose foot and with a zigzag stitch overcast the cut edge to keep it from fraying in the wash. Then press firmly on an ironing board.

you know the secret of your original jean hem.

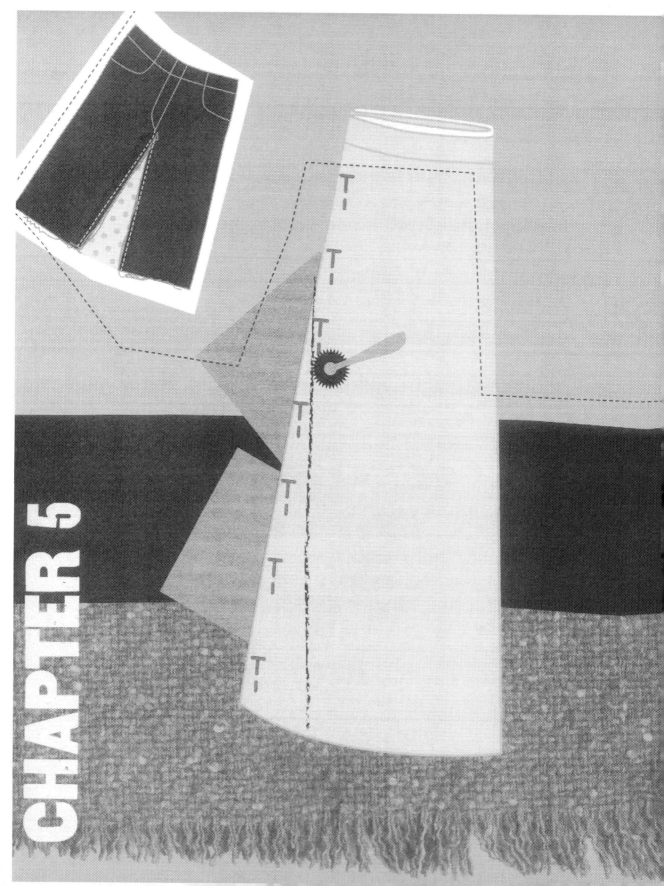

CHAPTER 5

Skirts

sparkly cuff, see page 152

ruched skirt, see page 138

The styling of skirts has gone through so many radical changes since the early 1900s Gibson girl look with the separation of the dress into a skirt, from 1920s flappers to 1930s glamour to the 1940s when skirts made their debut in uniforms to the 1960s mod miniskirts to today, when anything goes. There even have been theories about our economy relating to skirt lengths! Long, short, very old or brand-new, the potential for a fabulous deconstruct and reconstruct may be in your closet now. You will certainly come up with exciting reconstructed styles of your own by trying out some of the techniques in this chapter.

The Classic Jeans Skirt

Year after year the classic jean skirt never seems to die. Sometimes the trend is a long skirt and other times very short, and sometimes they have appliques or beading, or are dyed. This is perfect for that pair of jeans you have that have never looked quite right on you and been exiled to the back of your closet.

Use either a pair of blue jeans or corduroy jeans to convert them into a jean skirt. For inserts in the front and back of an ankle length skirt, use the leftover jean legs or 1 yard of fabric.

1. Put on your jeans and place your tape measure just under the waistband. Measure down to the finished length you want your skirt to be. A mid-thigh length or mini is about 14 inches from under the waistband, knee

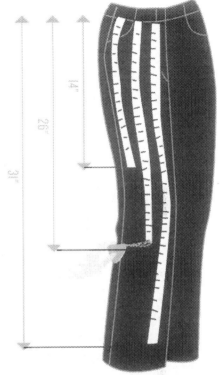

length is 26 inches long, and ankle length is 31 inches long. It's always good to be on the safe side, so chalk mark the pants 3 inches longer than the desired finished length.

2. *Lay the pants flat on a table and draw a horizontal line across each pant leg at the finished length you marked. Now cut off the excess pant legs and save them in case you want to use these pieces to insert into the skirt front and back.*

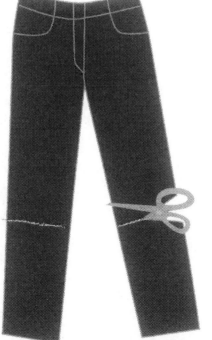

3. Use a seam ripper to open up the inseams on both legs of your jeans. The inseams are located on the inside of the legs and go up to the crotch seam of both sides of the jean. In the front crotch seam, rip open approximately 2 inches, starting at the opened inseams and work up toward the zipper. In the back crotch seam, rip open up toward the waistband approximately 3 inches.

4. Lay the jeans on a table with the front facing you. You may have to open the front crotch a little more to get it to lie flat on the table. Overlap the left side of the crotch on top of the right side and pin it down. Then flip the jeans onto the back and do the same thing.

5. Using your sewing machine, sew the pieces of the crotch down to the inseam, following the crotch line. Make sure not to sew the front to the back when you put this part of your jeans into the sewing machine.

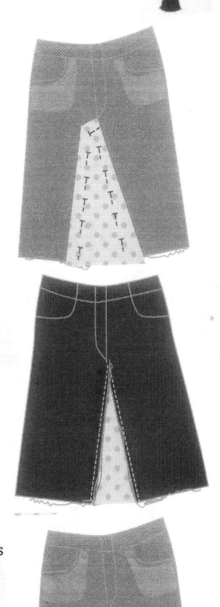

6. *Now for the triangular insert. To fill in the front and back to convert your jeans into a skirt, use either the leftover legs of the jeans or some other fabric.*

7. *On a table with your pants lying flat, carefully pin the fabric for the inserts onto the wrong side, where the open space is. Adjust the fabric to lie flat in the open space.*

8. *Sew on the right side of the skirt, following the edge of the opened jeans.*

9. *After the inserts are sewn in, on the wrong side of the skirt cut away the leftover fabric from the these pieces, but leave at least $\frac{5}{8}$-inch seam allowance. You can leave the hem unfinished, or you can make a hem on your new jean skirt by folding up the bottom of the skirt towards the wrong side 1 inch and then bending in the raw edge for a clean finish. Press the hem in place and then sew this edge by machine.*

And you don't have to stop there—turn this classic into an arty one-of-a-kind by adding sequins, fringe, gathers, racing stripes, or ruffles. Try these—and remember that they'll work on any kind of skirt, not just one made out of denim.

134

MATERIALS

- ¼ yard of sequined material
- straight pins
- marking chalk or pencil
- clear ruler
- scissors
- embroidery scissors
- fusible mending tape
- all-purpose thread
- sewing machine
- iron and ironing board
- sharp or between needle if hand sewing

Framing Using a Sequin Patch

This technique looks like a little window in your fabric and is another way to apply a patch, only this time you'll actually be patching a hole you've made.

1. Put on your skirt or lay it on a table to decide the placement of your framed patch.

2. Using a pencil, lightly draw a small rectangle shape approximately 3 inches long by 2 inches wide. Inside this rectangle, draw in another rectangle ¼ inch smaller on each side for your actual cutting line. Cut out the inner line and clip the four corners just a little.

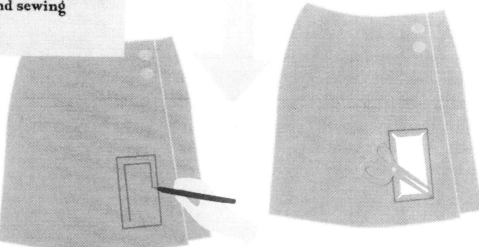

3. Turn under this ¼-inch line so that it forms the rectangle that is 3 inches by 2 inches and press at the ironing board. This is the frame for the sequin fabric patch.

4. Cut a rectangular patch 4 inches by 3 inches out of your sequinned fabric.

5. On the wrong side of the skirt, pin the sequin patch or fabric piece to cover the cut out rectangular shape. Make sure the right side of the sequin fabric is facing the wrong side of the skirt. Go to the ironing board and steam press, using fuse tape in between the rectangle and the sequin patch. Iron the patch in place, making sure the fuse tape has glued the sequin patch to the skirt. You can also sew around the rectangular frame by machine or by hand even after pressing the patch in place with fuse tape.

Fringe the Hems of Any Cutoff Skirt—Even an Old Wool Skirt

MATERIALS

- skirt made of woven material cut on the straight grainline
- one pin or needle
- scissors
- all-purpose thread to match your skirt
- sewing machine

Fringe is a form of embellishment used on scarves, western jackets, T-shirts, jean shorts and jean skirts, and other places. You can create it by unraveling any woven fabric so long as it's cut on the straight grain, not on the bias.

1. *If the skirt has a hem, cut it off at the fold up line to get a raw edge.*

2. *Sew by machine using a standard straight stitch or small zigzag stitch around the bottom of the skirt at the point you want the fringe to stop or approximately 1 inch up from the bottom. This will stop any fraying past where you want it frayed.*

SKIRTS

3. *Start by taking a pin to separate and pull out the woven crossgrain threads. Continue to pull them out and unweave them from the bottom of your skirt. Keep pulling out the crossgrain threads until you have a frayed edge the width you like. If the frayed edge is uneven, you can trim down the uneven threads of the fabric.*

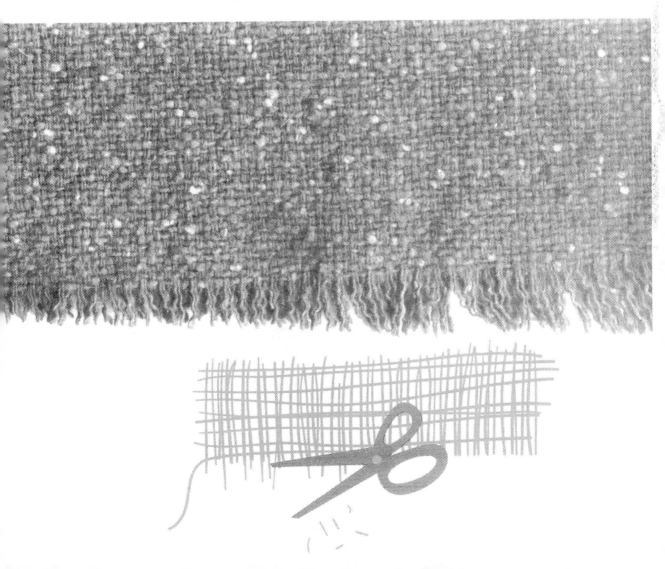

Using Elastic for a Gathered, or Ruched, Effect

An old skirt can be updated with a cluster of ruches, or small gathers, placed at a random point from the hemline up.

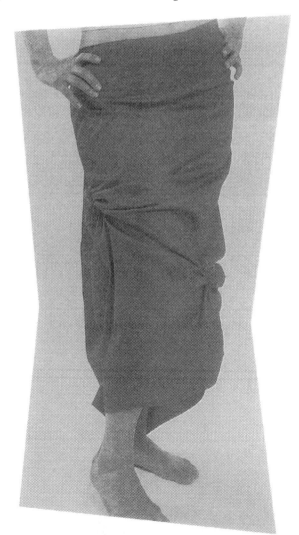

1. In front of a mirror, pin the places where you want the gathers.

2. Take the skirt off and turn it inside out. Chalk mark where you placed the pins and using a clear ruler draw a line over the chalk marks.

3. Take a measurement of the chalk line and cut a strip of ½-inch elastic 3 inches shorter than the measurement. Pin the end of the elastic at one end of the chalk marked line.

4. Set the straight stitch length on your sewing machine to the longest stitch length (approximately 4). Begin sewing the elastic to the chalk line. As you sew, pull back gently with one hand on the elastic and with your other hand stretch the elastic toward you as much as you can while sewing it to cover the chalk line. As you are pulling the elastic it will begin to create gathers in the fabric that you are sewing it onto. Be patient when first doing this technique since it takes a little bit of practice.

Add Twill-Tape Racing Stripes

Twill tape is a cotton tape that is woven in a V pattern, and you can use it to add sporty racing stripes at the side seam or hemline of a plain skirt. It usually comes in widths of ½, ¾, or 1 inch, and typically the color is natural, though sometimes you can find it in black and colors, too. (Wrights is a brand that is easy to find at your local fabric store.)

MATERIALS

- skirt
- straight pins
- scissors
- twill tape
- clear ruler
- all purpose thread to match twill tape
- sewing machine

1. Pin the tape down flat to the side seams of your skirt and then cut off the excess.

2. At the starting end and bottom hem of the skirt, bend the twill tape under ½-inch for a clean finish.

3. Sew the twill tape down along the very edge of each side of the tape using a sewing machine. Sewing with a medium-size zigzag stitch can add to the look. If sewing by hand, use a small hand-basting stitch or backstitch.

SKIRTS

Add Velvet Ribbons

Horizontally placed velvet ribbons can add a rich and baroque look to a skirt that needs a simple makeover. Velvet ribbons come in many sizes from $3/16$ of an inch wide to more than 2 inches wide.

1. *Measure evenly up from the skirt hem as you pin or chalk mark all around the circumference of the skirt. Then pin the ribbon onto the chalk line.*

2. *Using a sewing machine on the edge of each side of the ribbon, sew the ribbon onto the skirt using the same technique outlined for the twill-tape racing stripes.*

- skirt
- enough velvet ribbon to cover the circumference of your skirt where you want it placed, plus 2 inches
- straight pins
- marking chalk or pencil
- clear ruler
- scissors
- all-purpose thread to match the ribbon
- sewing machine
- sharp or between needle if hand sewing

Tapering a Full Skirt into a Pencil Skirt

MATERIALS

- **full skirt**
- **straight pins**
- **marking chalk or pencil**
- **clear ruler**
- **scissors**
- **seam ripper**
- **tracing paper**
- **tracing wheel**
- **all-purpose thread to match the skirt**
- **sewing machine**
- **iron and ironing board**
- **sharp or between needle if hand sewing**

Sometimes a skirt just needs some extra taper to make it the sexy skirt you thought it was when you bought it. (This can be done to pant and jean legs too.)

1. *Put on the skirt and stand in front of a mirror to decide how much to take in the side seams. With safety pins or straight pins, pin the amount you want to taper on just one side seam. Pinch in with your fingers and then pin starting from the hemline going up the skirt until you reach just below your hipline.*

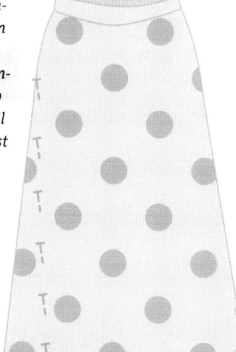

2. *Take off your skirt and lay it down on a table. Before drawing the new taper line, use a seam ripper to open up the hem on both side seams of the skirt enough to pull it down—that way you can draw your new taper line starting at the very bottom of the hemline. Then turn your skirt to the wrong side and rub marks over the pins with the marking chalk.*

3. *Take out the pins. With the clear ruler join the chalk marks to create one continuous line that blends into the hip of the original sewn seam line on your skirt.*

4. *To transfer the new taper line to the other side of the skirt, fold the skirt in half, making sure to match the original sewn side seams. Pin the two side seams together and then slide a piece of tracing paper underneath all four pinned-together seams. With a tracing wheel (press hard) trace the chalk-marked taper line onto the other side of the skirt.*

5. *Unpin the folded skirt and sew up your new taper lines on both sides of it. Start from the bottom and sew into the original side seams at the hip line, following the traced chalk line.*

6. *Try the skirt on again to see how you like the newly sewn taper line. Trim off the excess from the side seams by carefully marking a ⅝-inch cutting line from the new taper line. Using an iron, press this new taper line and then press the hem back up. A quick hand-sewn blind hem will keep the hem of the skirt in place. Steam press the new tapered side seams.*

Turn an Old Dress into a New Skirt

You might have an old dress tucked away that you stopped wearing since it's just not in style anymore. But by making it into a skirt you can bring it back to life again. I once found a beautiful taffeta and velvet party dress in the Salvation Army for $15, cut off the dated velvet top part, and made it into a really stylish skirt to wear to cocktail parties. All you need is the kind of dress where the top is sewn to the skirt at the waistline—that way you can easily separate them.

1. *Open up the waistline seam where the top meets the skirt with your trusty seam ripper. When you do this, be very careful not to take out any gathers or shirring that were sewn onto the waistline. Usually the skirt fullness is held in place with an extra sewn stitch line. Try not to cut this stitch line, just the one that will separate the bodice part from the skirt. Some*

MATERIALS

- old dress
- 1 yard of 7/8-inch-wide grosgrain ribbon for the waistband, preferably to match dress
- straight pins
- scissors
- seam ripper
- all-purpose thread to match your dress
- sewing machine
- iron and ironing board
- sharp or between needle if hand sewing
- optional: snaps

dresses a have a zipper in the side seam or the center back seam. You can cut the zipper off at the waistline or replace it by sewing in snaps, since this side opening is needed to pull the skirt up over your hips, which I'll show you how to do in a later step.

2. The raw edges of your separated skirt now need to be finished off with a zigzag stitch on your sewing machine.

3. To attractively cover the semi-unfinished waistline and any gathering there, pin the grosgrain ribbon on top of the waist on the right side of the skirt. At each end of the open waistline, bend the grosgrain ribbon in toward the wrong side *of the* skirt and pin it in place.

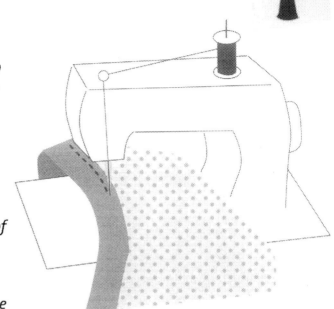

4. *Sew the grosgrain ribbon to the waistline of the skirt by placing it into the sewing machine on the right side. To make a clean finish, be sure to sew on the edge of the grosgrain so that is overlapping the waistline of the skirt. This will make a clean finish.*

5. *When sewing snaps into the side or center back seams, place one on the grosgrain waistband and then space the others approximately 1½-inches apart. Using your iron, press the grosgrain ribbon and the skirt opening.*

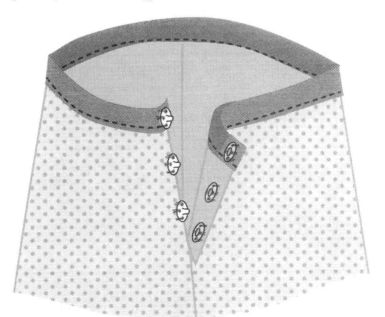

CHAPTER 6

Accessories

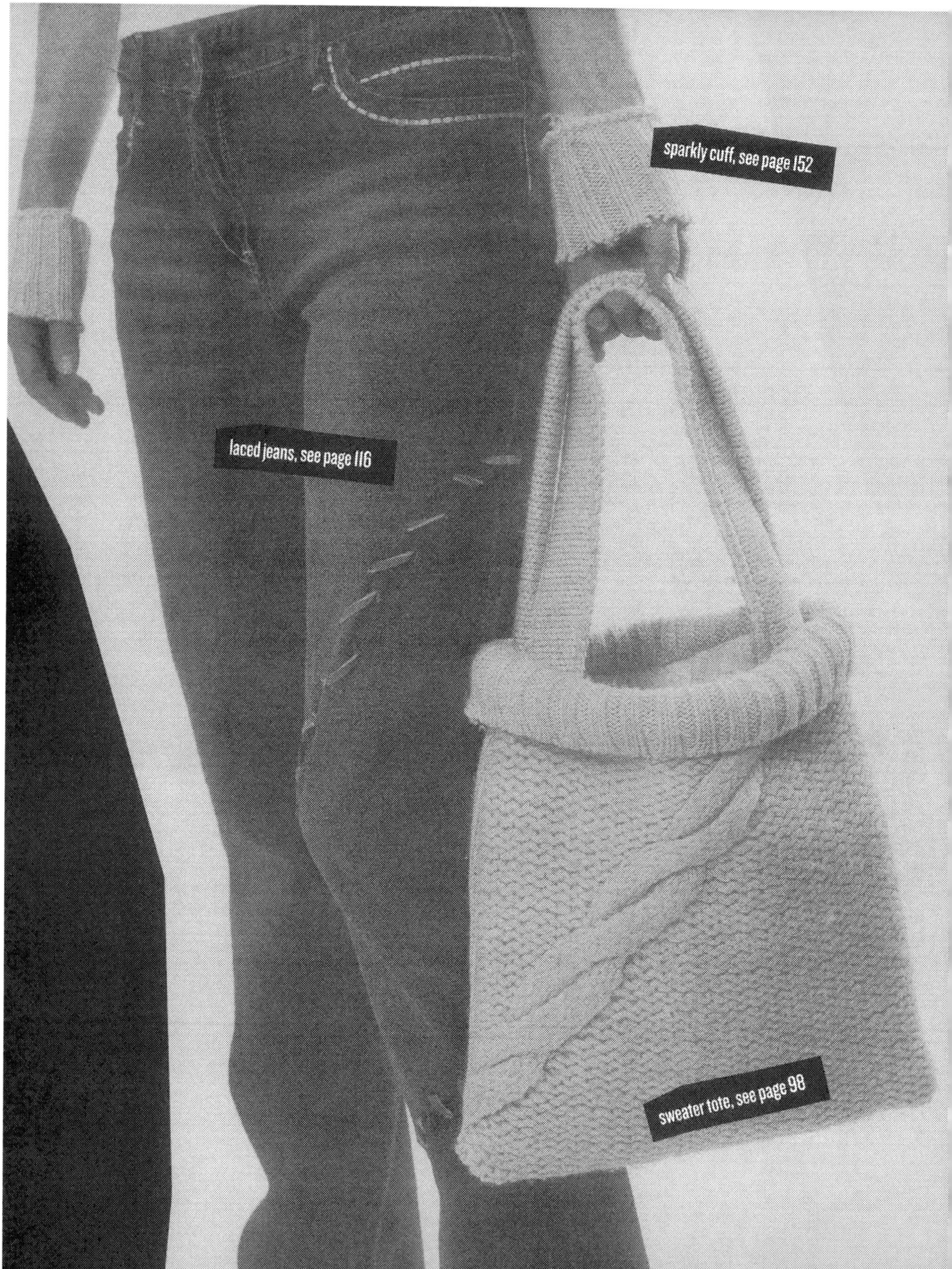

sparkly cuff, see page 152

laced jeans, see page 116

sweater tote, see page 98

Accessories add extra pizzazz to whatever you're wearing. This chapter shows you how to make several fast and easy accessories that can be put together in just a few hours.

Sparkling Armbands and Bracelets

You can make an armband or bracelet out of the cut-off ribbing from one of the sweatshirts, T-shirts, or sweaters you've already sliced and diced. First, try on the rib cuff to see if it stays in place on your arm or that it fits wherever you want to wear it.

Otherwise, you should make it tighter by taking it in either by hand or machine. Always make sure there is enough stretch to slip the rib cuff over your hand. Once you have the cuff fitted, it's time to decorate it. A fun way to do that is with beads, which you can get at sewing stores, craft stores, and even local boutiques that sell nothing but beads. They come in all shapes, sizes, and colors, so you can really express yourself with them.

One way of doing this is to arrange the beads in a cluster and mark their placement on the cuff with a pencil. Then all you need is a beading needle (or sharp) and all-purpose thread. Sew the beads and sequins onto the cuff. When sewing, don't pull the thread too tightly since you need slack to allow for stretch when slipping the cuff over your hand. The slack in the thread can remain on the inside of the cuff.

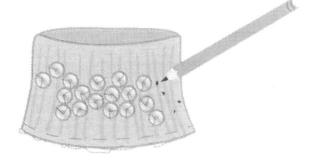 

Another style of beading involves long strings of beads hanging from the rib cuff. For this style you'll need a sharp needle or beading needle and button and carpet thread. Thread your needle so the length of the single thread is approximately 36-inches long. Sew one end of the thread to the end of the rib cuff and securely knot it in place. You can do this with an actual knot or by going back over your sewn thread several times. Then allow 5½ inches of thread to hang off the rib cuff. Thread the beads to look like a hanging strand. When threading the last bead, wrap the thread around the outside of the bead and then slide the thread back through all the beads. Lock this thread in a knot next to the one you started the strand with. Keep making these strands of beads one alongside the other, approximately ½-inch apart on the cuff. Varying the lengths of the beads also looks nice.

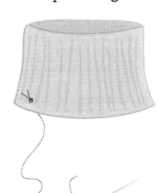 

Old neckties have been made into everything from vests to handbags, so why not belts? Instead of just pulling a necktie through the belt loops of your pants or skirts and knotting it, you can make a simple belt by using D-rings (metal rings in a D shape) for a more refined look. D rings are usually sold at fabric or craft stores.

MATERIALS

- standard man's tie
- pair of D rings, ¾ to 1 inch wide
- scissors
- all-purpose thread to match your dress
- iron and ironing board
- sharp needle for hand sewing

1. *All ties are made with an overlapped finish in the center back of the tie, with a loose basting stitch and thick interfacing keeping the tie in shape. Open the basting stitch at least 16-inches, starting from the end of the widest part of the tie. Then remove and cut away the interfacing up to the 16-inch point.*

2. *Turn the tie sideways so that it is folded in half with the basting stitch on the side. Carefully press the tie flat sideways. Now slip the D rings onto the narrow end of the tie and adjust them by pulling the narrow end of the tie. Your belt should be approximately 54-inches long from the D rings to the point of the tie. Cut off the rest of the narrow part of the tie, leaving enough to bend back to make a clean finish, and sew the D rings in place.*

3. *Use a hand backstitch to secure the D rings to the end of the tie.*

You can also use D rings with ribbon to make a belt. Keep in mind that these make great gifts for friends!

Making a Bustier Belt

- three lengths of 1½-inch-wide black elastic that are the same measurement as your waist
- ¼ yard of black fabric
- ¼ yard of fusible interfacing
- 1½ yards of ¼-inch-wide ribbon
- Dritz eyelet kit
- safety pins
- straight pins
- marking chalk or pencil
- clear ruler
- tape measure
- scissors
- embroidery scissors
- black thread
- sewing machine
- iron and ironing board
- sharp or between needle if hand sewing

A bustier is a simplified version of a corset, which is carefully constructed with boning and meant to pull the waist in as

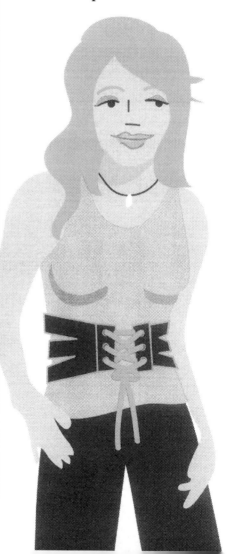

well as lift the bustline. A bustier will not perform the function that a corset does; however this design of a bustier belt is my way of blending a good fit *and* a good look. It's such an interesting design that you can wear it around your hips as well as on and above your waist.

1. *Measure your waist and subtract three inches. Cut the three rows of elastic to this measurement.*

2. *At each end of the elastic pieces, place the three strips together with two on top and the center elastic underneath. Pin them to hold them in place so the elastics measure 3½-inches wide at each end. Sew the three strips of elastic together at each end to secure them.*

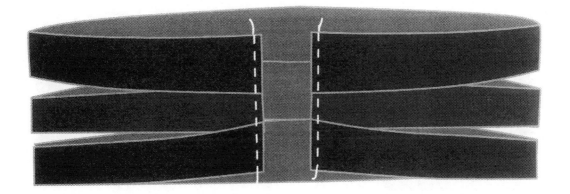

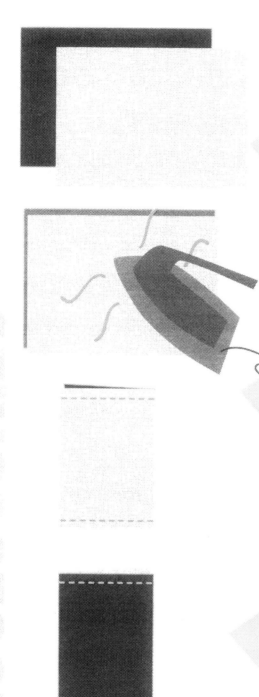

3. To make the fabric ends of the belt, measure and cut out two rectangular pieces of black fabric 5-inches long by 4½ inches wide (includes ½-inch seam allowance). Cut the fusible to the same size.

4. With an iron, steam press the fusible onto the wrong side of the cut pieces and then press the pieces in half on the right side. Now turn the pieces to the wrong side and sew the 2-inch sides closed using ½-inch seam allowance.

5. After sewing, turn to the right side. Push the corners out gently with the tips of your scissors. Press very carefully with the iron. On the open side, press in the ½-inch seam allowance. You now have the two fronts for your belt.

6. Insert each of the sewn strips of elastic into the fabric fronts ends. Push the elastic ½ inch in and pin it to hold in place. Adjust the zigzag stitch on your  sewing machine to the widest width and the stitch length to 4—this will enable you to sew through all thicknesses. Sew the fabric fronts to the elastic ends using the zigzag stitch. At the center back of your belt, sew through all three elastic strips. For a real finished look, use the iron to press the fabric ends.

7. With marking chalk or a pencil, evenly space your eyelets three on each side of the fabric pieces. The center of the eyelet should be ½-inch from the folded 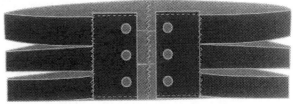 fabric pieces. With embroidery scissors, poke a hole for the eyelets. Follow the instructions for attaching the eyelets. Once the eyelets are in place, thread the ribbon through to lace up the belt. Try on your new belt and cut off any excess ribbon.

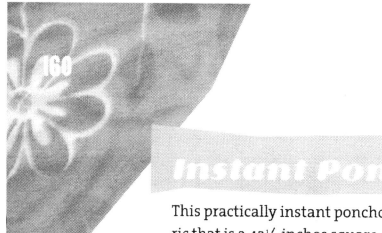

Instant Poncho

This practically instant poncho can be made from fabric that is a 42½-inches square, or you can make a smaller poncho out of a standard-sized scarf (32-inch square).

MATERIALS

- 1¼ yards of fabric at least 45 inches wide (silks, chiffons, georgettes, loosely woven animal fibers such as mohair, and knits are best), or a scarf 32 inches square
- straight pins
- marking chalk or pencil
- clear ruler
- scissors
- all-purpose thread to match your fabric
- sewing machine
- iron and ironing board
- sharp or between needle if hand sewing

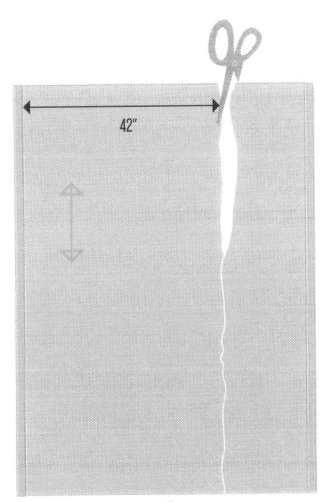

42"

1. *Prepare the fabric by marking the cross grain at 42½-inches. Clip into the fabric and tear down lengthwise to remove the excess. Lay the fabric flat on a table. Fold over the cross grain of the fabric to meet the lengthwise grain so you create a triangle. With scissors, trim off the remaining length of fabric.*

2. To create the neckline, fold the triangle in half again by folding it point to point. Chalk mark the center of this fold line. Then on each side of the center mark, draw a line 5½ inches long for the neckline. For front neckline, mark ½ inch at the centerfold. Then draw another line meeting up at the ends of the first line.

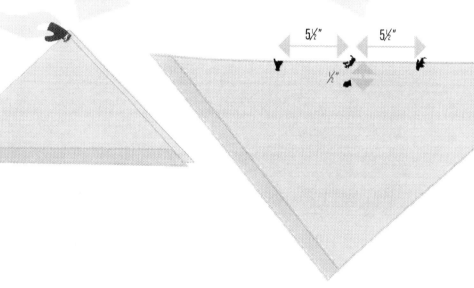

5½"   5½"

½"

3. With scissors, cut this line open. Carefully press under the raw edges all around the cut neckline to the wrong side with either a double-folded or single-folded edge. To finish the neckline, you can hand sew using a small blind hemstitch, or machine sew with a straight stitch or zigzag stitch. Be very careful not to stretch this neckline since it is on the true

bias. After
sewing the neck-
line, steam press it in
place.

4. Finishing the sides of the
poncho can be done the same
way as the neckline. If you used a
scarf, you won't even have to finish
the edge, since it's already done. But
there are many other ways to finish the
poncho—you can sew on decorative trims with
beading and fringe; press and sew a small double-
folded finish; or—my favorite—sew on double-fold
bias tape. Typically used around edges of place mats
and potholders, double-fold bias tape comes in
many colors and can be found
in fabric stores. It comes
packed, pressed and double
folded with one side folded
slightly wider than the
other. A bias tape foot for
your machine makes it
easier to sew, but it
can be done by
hand too.

¼ or ½ wide, double
fold bias tape

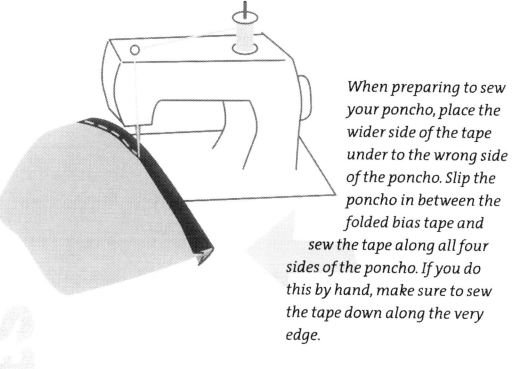

When preparing to sew your poncho, place the wider side of the tape under to the wrong side of the poncho. Slip the poncho in between the folded bias tape and sew the tape along all four sides of the poncho. If you do this by hand, make sure to sew the tape down along the very edge.

To finish, fold in raw edge of tape and sew to end of scarf corner

Make a Fabric Flower Pin to Adorn Your Poncho, T-Shirt, Sweater, or Bag

Flowers are blooming in fashion and are a great accent pinned on any garment—especially one of the ones you've just deconstructed and reconstructed! You can create them from bias strips that are cut, folded, and gathered together. You can even make this flower using bias strips cut from an old scarf.

MATERIALS

- ½ yard of fabric at least 45 inches wide (organdy, satin, silk, georgette, or lightweight cotton work best) or a scarf 32 inches square
- 1 safety pin
- marking chalk or pencil
- clear ruler
- scissors
- all-purpose thread to match your fabric
- sewing machine
- sharp or between needle if hand sewing

1. *To make bias strips, fold the cross grain of your fabric to the lengthwise grain. The 45-degree angle that is the fold is the true bias. Carefully cut the fold into two separate layers.*

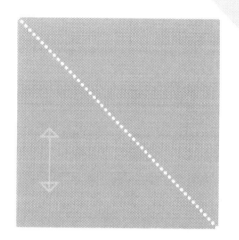

2. *With a ruler, measure and mark out strips of bias that are 5 inches wide and 25 inches long. Fold the bias strip in half.*

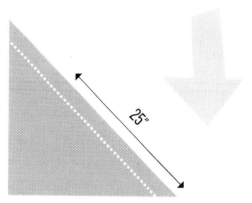

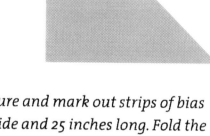

25"

3. *Adding some gathers will help make your flower take shape. You can do this by hand or on your sewing machine. On the machine, set your stitch length to the longest stitch and start sewing the folded bias strip ½ inch in from the cut edge and from one end to the other.*

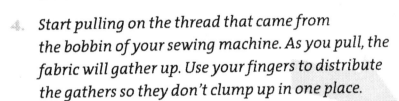

4. *Start pulling on the thread that came from the bobbin of your sewing machine. As you pull, the fabric will gather up. Use your fingers to distribute the gathers so they don't clump up in one place.*

5. *To shape your flower, start from one end of the bias strip and curl the fabric around and around like a coil and it will begin to take on the appearance of a big flower. By just cutting down the amount of fabric, you can make the flower the size you want.*

6. *Safety pin the bottom of the flower to hold it in place. Using a needle and thread, sew the bottom part with a stitch going through all the fabric. Sew back and forth until you feel the flower is securely held together.*

Now that you've made one, you can get started on a whole garden!

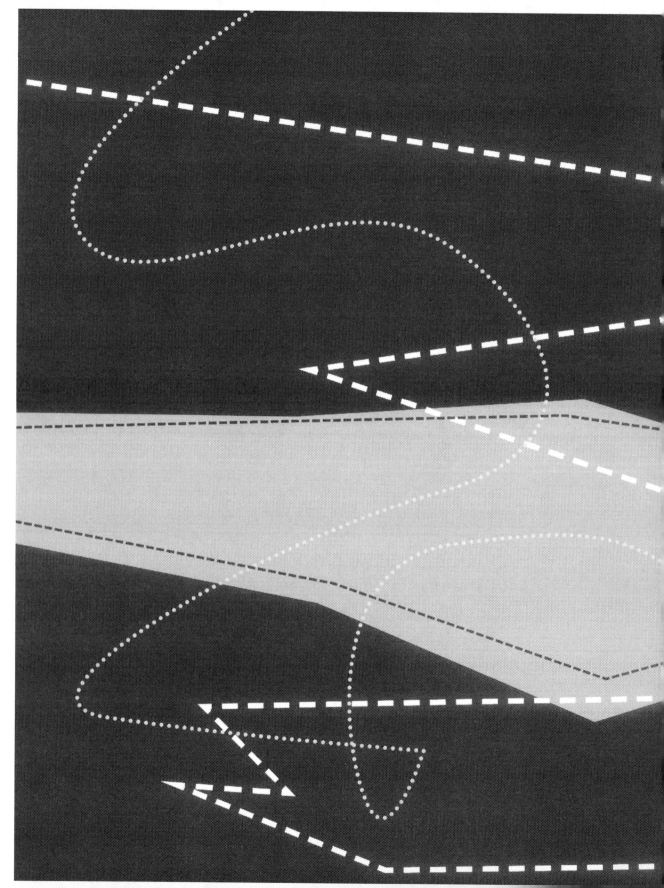

Glossary

ALL-PURPOSE FOOT—The foot on your sewing machine that is used generally for all sewing projects. You can change this foot to other feet for special purposes, such as sewing in a zipper.

APPLIQUÉ—A decoration that is sewn, glued, or fused to another fabric.

A-LINE—A silhouette shape of a simple skirt, fitted at the top and flaring wider at the hemline.

BACKSTITCH OR BACK TACK—A reverse stitch on the sewing machine to keep the sewn seam from opening.

BASTING—A temporary stitch usually made by hand to hold two fabrics together while sewing them by machine.

BEESWAX—Helps keep hand-basting thread from getting knotted. Pull the thread along the beeswax to get a coating of the beeswax.

BIAS—The bias cut is the softest, drapeiest way a fabric can hang. To achieve bias the fabric must be folded so that the lengthwise grain matches to the crosswise grain. The fold line becomes the true bias.

BIAS TAPE—Cut strips made from the bias cut of fabric. Used to finish a raw edge and it is very easy to sew this tape around corners.

BLIND HEM—A hand stitch that doesn't show on the right side of the garment and keeps the hem in place. Blind hems can be made on a sewing machine if there is a stitch setting for it, though you'll need a blind hem foot.

BOBBIN—A small round spool of thread that inserts into the sewing machine in order to make the machine sew.

BOLT—Unit in which fabric is packaged by the manufacturer and sold to fabric stores.

CALENDARING—A finishing technique on fabric used to polish the fabric with a shiny, lustrous finish. Some cotton fabrics have this finish.

CASING—A folded-over edge of a garment or a tunnel of fabric through which a drawstring cord, elastic, or ribbon is pulled. It is usually on pants or skirts and backpacks.

CLEAN FINISH—any method (zigzag stitch, overlocked, or turned under) used to finish the raw edges of a garment piece, usually on hems and facings.

CLIP—A small cut with the tips of scissors into the seam allowance of fabric. Used to mark notches or help release strain on curved seams such as necklines.

CORD STOP—A small plastic device that locks a drawstring in place.

CORDING—A decorative piping with a cotton cord filling. It is usually sewn into the edge of a pillow and used as trim in the seams of clothing.

CROSS GRAIN—The threads that run horizontally across the fabric from selvage to selvage. Also called the weft.

DARNING—Act of repairing small holes, rips, and worn areas in fabric by hand sewing though it can sometimes be done with a sewing machine.

DARTS—A triangle that tapers to a point and fits fabric to the curve of the body. Usually seen on the side seam of blouses or on skirts, pants, and dresses to create shape.

DRAPE—How fabric hangs. Depending on the thickness, sheer quality, fiber content, and how the fabric is cut will determine the way fabric hangs.

DECORATIVE STITCHES—Many sewing machines have decorative stitches that can create a design effect on a project you're sewing. Experiment with them to see the effects.

EASE—Slightly extra fullness added to a sewing pattern to allow for movement.

EDGE STITCH—A sewn line that is $\frac{1}{16}$ inch in from the edge of the fabric.

TOP STITCH—A sewn stitch line on the top of fabric used for decorative or functional purposes.

EDGING—Narrow decorative border of lace or embroidery trim. It is sewn on top of the raw edge of the fabric. Can be used to finish off raw edges of T-shirts, skirts, and pants.

FACE OF FABRIC—A textile term that means the right side of the fabric. Some fabrics are woven so it's difficult to tell which is the right or wrong side. Always chalk mark the wrong sides of anything you cut out. This will keep you from mixing them up.

FACING PIECE—A layer of fabric that is folded back to the inside so as to keep from having a raw edge showing.

FELLED SEAMS—A double-sewn seam that is usually used to sew the side seams of jeans and men's tailored shirts, which creates a clean finish.

FLOUNCE—A ruffle that is attached to a garment as trim.

FOLD LINE—The exact center of a pattern. A symbol of this appears on most patterns.

FOLD SYMBOL—A bracket arrow indicating the fold line of a pattern.

FUSIBLE FABRIC—Fabric with glue backing that can be ironed onto other fabrics to give additional support and stiffness.

FUSE TAPE (OR FUSIBLE BUD WEB)—A tape that has glue on both sides used to glue two pieces of fabric together or mend a hole.

GATHER—To draw up fabric fullness on a line of stitching.

GRAIN—The threads that are woven into the length or warp of a fabric.

GROSGRAIN RIBBON—A strong, firmly woven ribbon with crosswise ribs. It can be used for decorative trim or as a waistband on a skirt.

HEM—Fabric that is turned in toward the wrong side of a skirt or pant and is sewn in place to finish off raw edges.

INTERFACING—A fusible fabric that is ironed onto garments or bags and belts that gives support in order to keep it from stretching out of shape.

JOIN—To stitch together the pieces of a pattern.

LENGTHWISE GRAIN—The threads, which run down the length of the fabric and are parallel to the selvage. This is also called the warp.

LOCK STITCH—The basic straight stitch made on a sewing machine.

NOTIONS—Small supplies used to make a garment such as pins, needles, and thread.

NAP—Some fabrics have a surface that when you rub your hand in one direction it will be one shade and if you rub in the opposite direction it will shade slightly different. Fabrics with nap are velvet, suede, corduroy, and fur.

OVERCAST STITCH—A hand stitch that is similar to an overedge stitch. It is used to finish off seams or for a decorative effect.

OVEREDGE STITCH—Used to cover and finish raw seams. This can be done on most home sewing machines with a zigzag stitch.

OVERLOCK STITCH—A special machine stitch that is used to sew knits. It is also seen on the seams of jeans and most garments in order to finish off raw edges.

PLACKET—Any finished opening on a garment. For example, where the zipper is sewn on jeans.

PIPING—A narrow strip of fabric folded on the bias and sewn in between seams for a decorative finish.

ROLLED HEM—A very small hem made to create a rolled edge.

ROTARY CUTTER—A cutting tool with a round blade that must be used with a cutting mat. It is great to use for cutting bias strips of fabric.

RUCHING—Gathering or pleating made out of fabric and sewn onto a garment for decoration.

SEAM—Where fabrics are joined together sewing by hand or machine.

SEAM ALLOWANCE—The fabric distance between the cutting line and sewing line of a pattern.

SEAM GUIDE—There are several seam guides made, but the best to get is a magnetic seam guide to help you sew straight seams.

SELVAGE—A woven or printed edge on each side of a woven fabric. Knits don't have this kind of edge. Instead, there are poked holes and a stiff finish on each end of the knit.

SEWING MACHINE FEET—Your sewing machine will generally come with different feet that snap on or screw on. Feet help you with sewing all sorts of stitches. For example, a zipper foot will help when sewing in zippers.

STAY STITCHING—A machine stitch that is used to keep fabric from stretching.

SKIRT HEM MARKER—A tool that has a ruler and marking powder so that you can mark a hemline for a skirt.

SEAM BINDING—A narrow woven tape like a ribbon used to cover the raw edge of a hem.

SHIRR—To gather up fabric into a ruffle.

TAILORS CHALK (OR MARKING CHALK)—A chalklike or waxlike substance used for general marking.

TOPSTITCH—A decorative stitch which is sewn ¼-inch away from the finished edge.

TUCK—A stitched fold at the waistline of skirts, pants, shirts, and jackets. Tucks add fullness to a garment.

VENT—A lapped opening or form of slit used at the hem of skirts, jackets, and coats.

WARP—Threads that run vertically or lengthwise in a woven fabric. Warp threads are the strongest part of the fabric.

WEFT—Threads that run horizontally or crosswise in a woven fabric. The weft part of a fabric is not as strong as the warp.

GLOSSARY

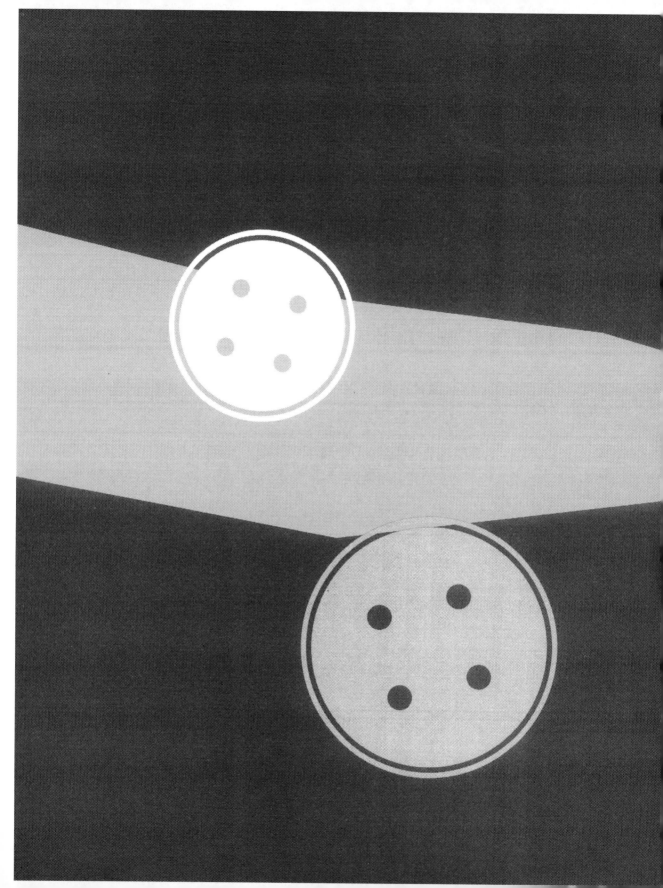

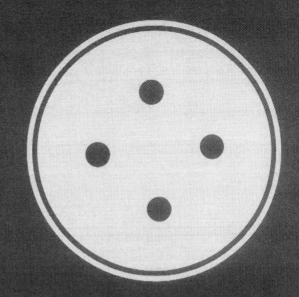

Resources

This is a resource list of great places to find all sorts of special items you may not find at Wal-Mart, Jo-Ann, or Michaels. Wal-Mart (www.walmart.com) carries sewing patterns by name brands, quilting and craft supplies, and sewing machines. Jo-Ann (www.joann.com) sells all sorts of sewing items for fashion sewing and home decor such as fabrics, trims, sewing supplies, patterns, some books, and craft supplies. They also sell sewing machines. Michaels (www.michaels.com) sell arts and crafts supplies.

For more specialized, unique goods, check out the following.

PATTERNS

Amazon Drygoods Ltd.
800-798-7979, 319-322-6800
411 Brady Street
Davenport, IA 52801
www.amazondrygoods.com
Large selection of patterns; catalog $7.

Folkwear Patterns
888-200-9099
www.folkwearpatterns.com
Vintage and folkwear patterns
www.sewingpatterns.com
Great Web site for ordering many different brands of sewing patterns.

Elan Pattern Company
979-758-3100
Fabric Depot
P.O. Box 411
Garwood, TX 77442
www.fabricdepot.com
Bra-making supplies and patterns. Kits. Catalog $3.

Kieffer's
201-798-2266
P.O. Box 7500
Jersey City, NJ 07307
Lingerie patterns, assorted stretch dance fabrics and supplies. A catalog is available.

FABRICS

Seattle Fabrics

206-525-0670

8702 Aurora Avenue N. (N. 87 Street)

Seattle, WA 98103

www.seattlefabrics.com

Outdoor and recreational fabric and hardware. Polartec and specialty fabrics, webbing, thread, and zippers.

Malden Mills retail store

877-289-7652

530 Broadway

Lawrence, MA 01841

www.maldenmillsstore.com

Polartec fabric

Fabulous-Furs

800-848-4650, 859-291-3300

601 Madison Avenue

Covington, KY 41011

www.fabulousfurs.com

Full line of faux fur fabrics, patterns, faux fur coat kits, and sewing notions.

Rose Brand

800-223-1624, 212-242-7554

75 Ninth Avenue

New York, NY 10011

www.rosebrand.com

Large stock of extra-wide seamless muslin and canvas, meant for scenery and theater.

RESOURCES

Thai Silks

800-722-7455, 650-948-8611
252 State Street
Los Altos, CA 94022
www.thaisilks.com
All kinds of silks; mail order, brochure.

La Lame, Inc

212-921-9770
250 West 39 Street
New York, NY 10018
www.lalame.com
Metallic prints, velvets, laces, and sequins.

Spandex House, Inc.

212-354-6711
263 West 38 Street
New York, NY 10018
www.spandexhouse.com
All types of stretch knit fabrics made out of spandex and Lycra.

Mood Fabrics Inc.

212-730-5003
225 West 37 Street, 3rd floor
New York, NY 10018
www.moodfabric.com
Great prices, Lots of different kinds of fabric as well as designer fabrics. The best in New York City.

Reprodepot Fabrics
www.reprodepotfabrics.com
Large selection of reproduction vintage fabrics on the Internet.

TRIMS AND HARDWARE

Wrights
877-597-4448
West Warren, MA 01092
www.wrights.com
Bias tape, webbings, and other craft supplies.

Dritz
www.dritz.com
Eyelets, grommets, D rings, nail heads, snaps, and every other notion under the sun.

Grey Owl Indian Crafts
800-487-2376, 732-775-9010
502 Atkins Avenue
P.O. Box 1185,
Neptune, NJ 07753
www.greyowlcrafts.com
Feathers and Native American beads and motifs.

RESOURCES

M&J Trimming Co.
212-391-6200, 212-842-5050
1008 Avenue of the Americas
New York, NY 10018
www.mjtrim.com
Buttons, buckles, beads, rhinestones, and handbag handles, as well as upholstery trims.

Daytona Trimmings Co.
212-354-1713
251 West 39 Street
New York, NY 10018
Laces, braid, and beaded trims, rickrack, snap tape, hook tape, emblems, sewing notions.

Fred Frankel & Sons, Inc.
212-840-0810
19 West 38 Street
New York, NY 10018
www.fredfrankel.com
Loose rhinestones, rhinestone bandings, pearls, beaded and sequined trims and motifs.

Kandi Corp.
www.kandicorp.com
Great Web site for all sorts of bling (rhinestones, studs, gems).

Hyman Hendler & Sons
212-840-8393
67 West 38 Street
New York, NY 10018
www.hymanhendler.com
Quality ribbons—grosgrain, satin, all types.

Mayer Import Co.

212-391-3810

25 West 37 Street

New York, NY 10018

www.mayerimport.com

Jewels, pearls, cameos, beads, etc.

Roth Import Co.

212-840-1945

13 West 38 Street

New York, NY 10018

www.rothinternational.net

Sequined and beaded appliqué, sequins and rhinestones by the yard, metallic braids and cords, beaded fringe.

Cartwright's

www.ccartwright.com

Sequins and vintage buttons.

Tinsel Trading

212-730-1030

47 West 38 Street

New York, NY 10018

www.tinseltrading.com

Ribbons trims, specializing in vintage metallics.

CRAFTS

Pearl Paint

800-723-2787

www.pearlpaint.com

Pearl Paint sells mostly art supplies and some craft supplies.

Dick Blick

www.dickblick.com

Online art supplies.

Rit

866-794-0800, 317-231-8028

www.ritdye.com

Dyes and fabric treatments.

Dharma Trading Co.

800-542-5227

P.O. Box 150916

San Rafael, CA 94915

www.dharamatrading.com

Dyes, paints, heat transfers, fabrics and garments for dying and quilting.

ACKNOWLEDGMENTS

I want to thank all my students and customers around the world as well as the gals and guys who work and teach in my place, since they are the ones who keep me on my sewing toes, looking for ways to make sewing interesting, creative, and new. I am always grateful to Mrs. Goldberg, my next-door neighbor when I was a child who encouraged all my curiosity about sewing, knitting, crocheting, and other crafts. My best friend, sweater designer Martha Weisberg, who passed away; my artsy friend Janice Harrison; critical eye artist friend Gale Leddy; Carl Raymond the visionary; Julie Benson, controller; Carole Jean Helms, my Parsons School design buddy; Lee Louie, patternmaker pal; Ann-Marie Langry, Emmanuel Duron, and Rejean Dorval, my French fashion posse; Peter Kolodney and Georges Nahitchevansky, my legal counsel. The biggest thanks to Gregory Garvin with his shining light of inspiration and encouragement all throughout the writing of this book for his young, quick, "I need to know it now" generation. Deborah Green who as always read my manuscript and remains supportive of my struggle to make things an

ACKNOWLEDGMENTS

easy and exciting read. Thank you to Georgia Rucker for her brilliant artwork and direction to make the book come to life. Amanda Patten, my editor, who taught me what it means to stand for my voice and style of writing. Thanks to my agent, Patty Moosbrugger, who smoothes over the drama queen in me. Thanks to James Livingston and Lisa Chaney, who taught above and beyond the call of duty so I could finish this book. And a special thanks to all the students who volunteered their time to pose for this book: Annie Arthur, Lena Selitzer, Elizabeth Durand, Azizi Johnson, Alison Frazer, Giovanna Mendez, Gregory Garvin, Heidi Nute, Melissa Gooch, and Michelle Casino. Thank you to my mother, the ninety-one-year-old miracle!